patch!

Cath Kidston

patch!

Cath Kidston

PHOTOGRAPHY BY PIA TRYDE

Quadrille
PUBLISHING

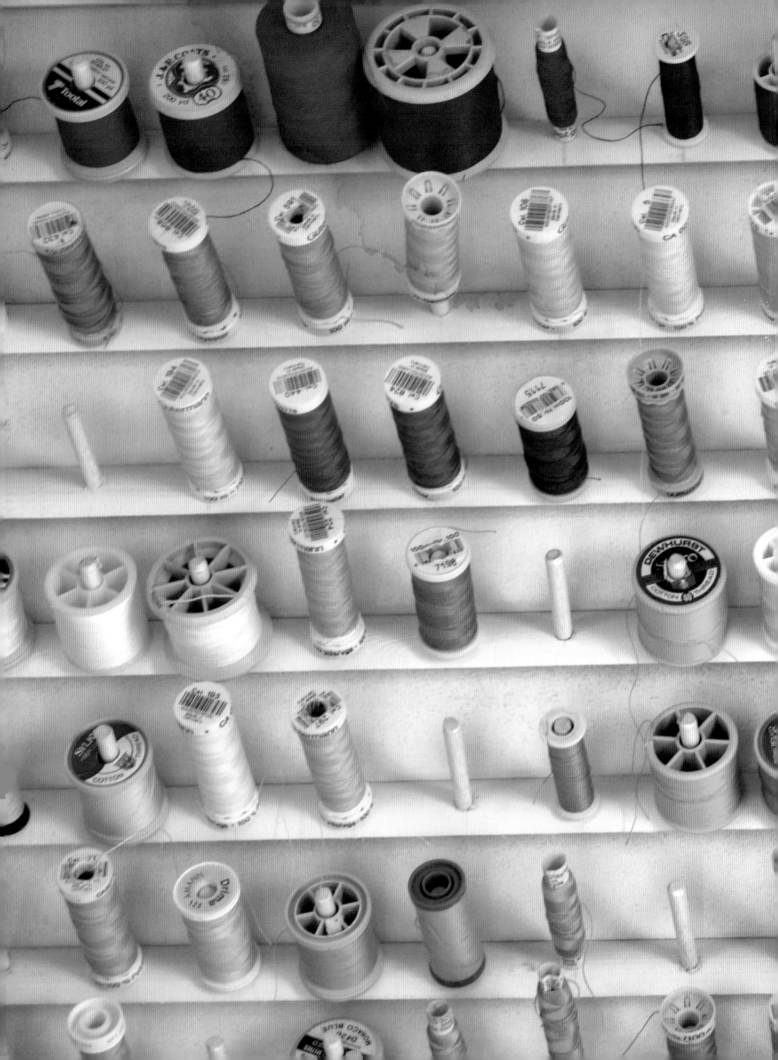

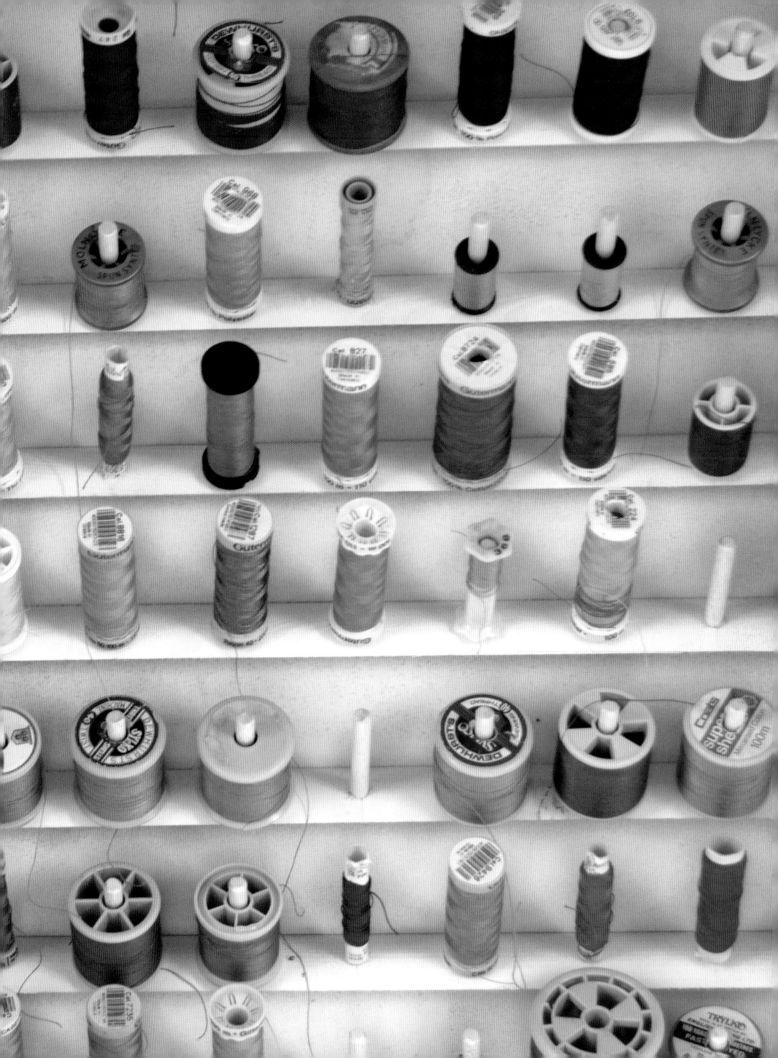

Introduction

Patch! is the fourth in my series of sewing books, and this time I've taken the title very literally. As anyone who's visited my stores will recognise, all my designs are about reinterpreting the past and taking a more contemporary, colourful approach to tradition. Once I started to explore the fascinating theme of patching and pieced work, I became inspired by the possibilities. I discovered a huge wealth of historic ideas, and I've come up with over thirty projects which bring a new twist to these versatile techniques.

Patchwork evolved as a thrift craft in an era when new fabrics were scarce and expensive, so it is right on trend with today's ethos of sustainability and recycling. It simply involves sewing together pieces of fabric to create a larger design, a technique which encompasses everything from meticulously hand-stitching dozens of tiny silk diamonds to running up an over-sized tablecloth from a bundle of vintage tea towels. I've enjoyed playing with these changes in scale and speed, and like the idea that whilst some of the projects will take many relaxing hours to stitch, others can be completed in an afternoon.

Appliqué is patchwork's sister craft, and instead of sewing the fabric together, cut-out shapes are sewn, or patched, on to a background. I've always felt like a virtuous homemaker when doing any domestic repairs, so I've even included some proper patching – a simple square on a worn-out knee. There are more involved techniques too, like the beautiful 'Hidden Circles' pattern used for the hand-appliquéd laundry bag on pages 58–61 and the intricate embroidered jigsaw of 'Crazy Patchwork' used on the cushion on pages 80–3.

I wanted to include something for everybody, so whatever your level of expertise, I hope you'll find a project that you'll enjoy making. My own first patchwork project was worked with paper templates, in English style, so maybe the Child's Pentagon Ball on pages 96–99 or the Hexagon Pincushion on pages 130–131 would make a good starting point for hand stitching. Moving on to machined patchwork, there's a range of pretty and practical bags, embellished garments and home accessories. You'll find cushions of all shapes and sizes, two full-size bedcovers, a curtain panel and a comfortable beanbag made out of plaid blankets.

The thrill of searching for vintage fabrics at boot sales and flea markets has long been one of my greatest pleasures, and I've always loved collecting textile scraps. Patchwork is the ideal way to use these: shirtings, silk scarves, dress prints, fine cotton, ticking and embroidered linen all appear alongside my own prints, and the more eclectic and unexpected the combination of fabrics, the better the result.

My intention in this book has been to broaden the boundaries of traditional patchwork and to take it back to its early roots by re-using fabric in innovative ways. Search through your ragbag for hoarded scraps, look through the following pages, and be inspired.

Cath Kidston

Patch! Basics

This introduction includes all the stitchery skills you'll need to create the projects, along with hints and tips on choosing equipment, using a sewing machine and finding fabrics, as well as some background to the various patchwork and appliqué techniques involved.

Essential Equipment

One of the best things about patchwork and appliqué is that you don't need any specialist equipment to get started: don't forget that all those wonderful antique quilts were made with nothing more complicated than fabric, scissors, thread and a needle or basic sewing machine. Here's a quick guide to all the tools and equipment that you'll need to make the projects in this book – the 'sewing kit' that appears in each materials checklist.

PINNING AND STITCHING

Keep all your hand-sewing needles together in the felt pages of a needle book, where they are easily visible – they do tend to get lost in the filling of a pincushion. They come in various lengths and thicknesses, from a chunky '1' down to a delicate size '10', each intended for a particular purpose. A mixed starter pack will contain:

• long 'embroidery' or 'crewel' needles, with narrow eyes to accommodate stranded threads

• medium-length 'sharps' for general use, which have small round eyes for sewing thread

• short 'betweens' or 'quilting' needles, slender enough to slip easily through several layers of fabric. These are also good for joining English-style paper patches but may prove too small for some stitchers.

A large safety pin or bodkin is useful for threading cords through gathering channels. Smaller safety pins are always handy and are good for temporarily securing layers of fabric. Fine (0.6mm) steel dressmaker's pins are suitable for cotton and other fine fabrics as they won't leave any marks, but I prefer longer glass-headed pins, which show up well, especially on woollens and patterned cloth. Store them safely in a tin or pincushion, but have a small magnet to hand in case they go astray.

MEASURING AND MARKING

All stitchers need an accurate tape measure, and if you're going to make quilts or curtains, an extra long one is invaluable. Use a 15cm ruler for checking seam allowances and hems. A sharp HB pencil is all you need for transferring markings and outlines, but you may prefer a dressmaker's pen. Use tailor's chalk or a chalk pencil on textured and darker fabrics.

CUTTING OUT

Invest in the best steel-bladed scissors you can afford and they'll last you a lifetime. Dressmaking shears are useful for cutting out large items, but smaller scissors are preferable for patches. Keep a spare pair of household scissors for paper and don't ever use your fabric scissors for templates or they will quickly become blunt! Embroidery scissors with sharp points will snip seams and threads efficiently. Most patchworkers also have a rotary cutter, quilter's ruler and a cutting mat – you can learn more about these overleaf.

SEWING AND TACKING

Stock up with spools of white and mid-grey thread for piecing several different fabrics and a couple of bright colours for tacking, so stitches are easy to spot and unpick. All-purpose sewing thread is good for hand or machine piecing. It comes in a wide range of colours – pick a slightly darker shade if you can't find an exact match for your fabric. If you also buy a thread plait, made from many short interwoven lengths, you'll always have the right colour for small sewing tasks.

ODDS AND ENDS

A well-stocked work basket contains one or more thimbles – essential if you're to avoid punctures when hand sewing. Silicone versions mould to your finger tip and are easier to use than traditional metal. Seam rippers look frightening with their sharp points but are indispensible for unpicking stitches when things go wrong. A lint roller is handy for picking up threads and slivers of fabric. Finally, an old-fashioned block of beeswax for strengthening thread adds sweet scent to your sewing kit.

Cutting Out

Whether you are preparing the front and back panels of a cushion cover or a stack of patches ready for a quilt, accurate measurement and precise cutting are essential if your completed project is going to have a professional finish with the pieces joined correctly together.

PAPER PATTERNS

If you are making up a bag, cushion or pillowslip, you'll need rectangular panels of various sizes for the straps, gussets, lining and backings, as well as the elements needed for the patchwork or appliqué. The dimensions for each panel are given in the 'cutting out' list for the project. When two measurements are given for a rectangular piece of fabric, the width measurement is always given first, then the length. Transfer these measurements on to dressmaker's pattern paper, which is ruled with a grid of centimetre squares, then cut out along the printed lines. Pin the patterns to your fabric and cut out around the outside edge with your largest scissors. When measurements are given for individual patches, as for the curtain or washbag, draw your pattern up on 1mm grid graph paper in the same way.

If you are making a large backing for a finished quilt, it's easier to lay the fabric out flat and pin the quilt top to it, then cut the edge. This way you'll know the two fit together exactly and there's no measuring up to do.

TEMPLATES

On pages 156–160 you'll find the templates required for many of the patchwork and appliqué projects, including several geometric shapes alongside the 'Dresden Plate' petals used in the bag and cushion. There is an appliqué Stanley and a couple of rabbits, plus the embroidery guide for the red work hens.

The geometric shapes are a pentagon for the child's toy ball on pages 96–99, a hexagon for the pincushion on pages 130–131 and a diamond for the Harlequin Bag on page 46–49. All of these are made using the English patchwork technique of stitching over paper templates. The best way to make the multiple templates needed is to photocopy the page on to thin card, then cut out the shape you need. Draw round this card shape on to scrap paper and old envelopes. You can make your own templates in other sizes by adjusting the size on your printer or by using a simple drawing programme on your computer, or with a bit of school day geometry, a ruler and a pair of compasses.

The outline template supplied for the Bunny Sweater on pages 140–141 is intended for iron-on appliqué, so all you have to do is to trace the reversed silhouette directly on to the paper side of the fusible bonding web. The motif for the Bunny Blanket on pages 104–105 and the Stanley appliqué for the Personalised Dog Bed on page 132–135 are stitched on to their backgrounds and so are the right way round. Trace them onto kitchen paper and cut out around the pencil line to make the templates.

GO WITH THE GRAIN

Press your fabric well before cutting out, to remove the creases. A light spray of starch or silicone fabric stiffener should get rid of any that are especially stubborn. Look at it hard and you'll see it's made up from two sets of interwoven threads which lie at right angles to each other. These are called the warp and weft, and the direction in which they lie is called the 'grain' of the fabric. You should always position your templates so that the straight edges lie parallel with one set of threads (along the grain), or the final patches will distort and pull when stitched together.

PLANNING YOUR PATCHES

If your fabric prints have an all-over, small-scale pattern the placement of the templates isn't important, because all the patches will be more or less the same. When working with stripes and checks, however, you should plan the positioning a little more carefully, so that one edges of the patch will be in line with the stripes or squares. You may also want the patches to be symmetrical or matching, which will require extra fabric.

Pick out individual motifs or flower sprays from other larger-scale or sprigged designs, centering them within the patch, as for the flowered silks for the Boudoir Cushion on pages 76–79 and the nursery prints on the Pentagon Ball on pages 96–99. If you make them all the same (known as 'fussy cutting') you can create some interesting effects. I did this with this Hexagon Pincushion and can just imagine how effective this would look repeated across the surface of a whole quilt!

Organise your prepared patches in zip-up sandwich bags, ready to be stitched, and if you're feeling really efficient, you can label them too.

ROTARY CUTTING

This relatively new innovation speeds the cutting out process, especially when making a large project like the Star Throw on pages 106–109 or the Curtain Panel on pages 114–117. It also enables you to cut several layers of fabric at once. Three separate tools are required:

• A rotary cutter, which acts like a very sharp pastry wheel. There are several types and sizes, but all have a round, rotating blade set in a handle. A 45mm diameter is best for patchwork. Check that it can be securely retracted to prevent accidents and always handle with care.

• A quilter's ruler, made from clear perspex and etched with a grid of centimetres or inches. The largest size, used for panels and extra large patches, is 15 x 60cm. Along with a 15cm square that is marked with 45 degree angle (for triangles), this should cover most of your needs. Glue small strips of fine sand paper to the back of the ruler to stop it slipping.

• A cutting mat, with a self-healing plastic surface. If you have space, get one to cover the table top. The extra expense is worth it in the long run.

There are two ways to rotary cut and it's a good idea to practise on some spare fabric first, to get the hang of the technique. For panels and larger patches, place the fabric on the mat and line up the ruler with the printed grid. Hold the cutter so that the blade is upright and lies against the ruler, then press down firmly and glide it away from you. Do the same, matching the ruler to the correct distance, on the other three sides.

You can also use the grid marked on the ruler to measure your patches. Line one corner up with the grain of the fabric and cut along these two edges. Turn the ruler the other way round, so that the lines that indicate your required size line up with the cut edges, then slice off the fabric from these two sides.

Machine Know-how

Only a few *Patch!* projects are stitched completely by hand. All the others involve an element of machine sewing, whether it's joining patches together, seaming a backing for a cushion or making an entire bag or pillowcase. Don't let this put you off if you're a novice stitcher. Nothing requires a great degree of technical knowledge and there's only one curved seam in the book... everything else consists of basic straight seams and hems and you'll learn how to do these on the following pages.

CHOOSING A MACHINE

Some patchworkers like to use antique hand-operated machines, preferring the accuracy and slow rhythmic pace produced by turning the handle. The basic straight stitch made by an old Singer is all you really need to join patches.

Modern machines, however, have a swing needle which moves from side to side to create zigzag and overlocking stitches. These are useful for neatening and strengthening raw seams and for edging appliqué patches. Any other functions are a bonus, so if you're buying your first machine don't be tempted to overspend on a digital model that links to your laptop. A solid entry-level machine (never the very cheapest, which often are not substantial enough to deal with heavier cloth) should get you started and you can always upgrade if you decide to do a lot of sewing.

THE TECHNICALITIES

All machines work in the same way by linking two threads – one on each side of the fabric – to produce an interlinked stitch. The upper reel is threaded under tension along the arm and down through the needle. The lower thread is wound onto a small bobbin housed in a case that is set into the flat bed. Take time to read through the manufacturer's manual to learn a bit more about how to use your individual machine and to get to know some technical terms.

These are the four main parts with which you should be familiar.

• The presser foot, as its name suggests, presses down on the fabric as it passes under the needle. It's operated by a small lever that lifts it up and down. It should always be lowered before you start stitching. You will need to change the pressure when sewing thicker fabrics, such as the blanket used for the dog bed, and the manual will tell you where to do this. Machines are supplied with several feet – you'll need just the basic one for all your seaming and the narrow zip foot when inserting a zip or sewing piping.

• The top end of the machine needle is attached to the arm and the upper thread passes through a hole in its tip. Like sewing needles, these come in different gauges and a 'universal' 70–80 should be fine when working with cotton fabrics. You'll need to adjust the needle's position when the zip foot is in place.

• The reverse stitch control is very useful. It enables you to work a few stitches in the opposite direction to the seam at both the beginning and end of the line. This stops the thread unravelling and strengthens the join.

• The flat throat plate has a small hole through which the needle passes to pick up the lower thread. It is engraved with a series of parallel lines: you can just see these on the photograph opposite. The adjacent figures indicate the distance between the needle and the line in millimetres, in other words, the width of the seam allowance.

LOOKING AFTER YOUR MACHINE

You'll need to do a bit of routine maintenance to keep your machine running smoothly. Always store it away in the carrying case or dust cover and oil occasionally as directed in the manual. Clear lint and dust from the bobbin case with the tiny brush supplied. It's a good idea to change the needle frequently as it will become blunt with use and cause the stitches to become irregular.

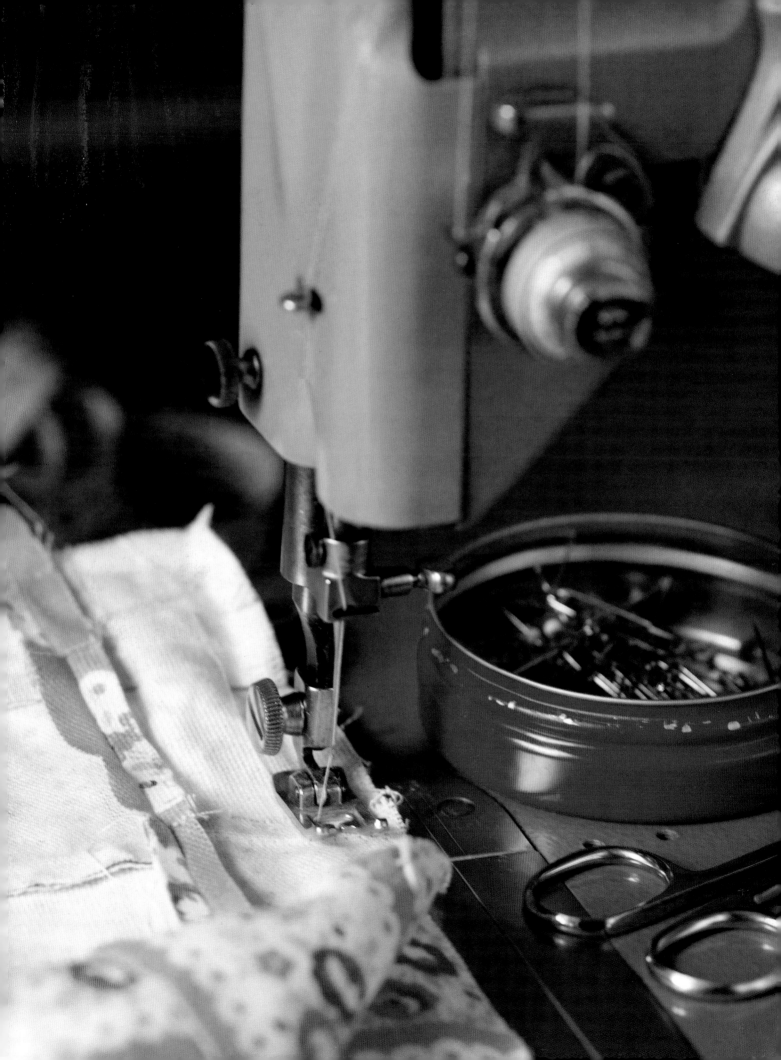

Sewing Basics

Any specialist patchwork and appliqué methods are explained in detail, with step-by-step illustrations, in the Patch! Projects section. Here's a quick tutorial covering the other basic sewing and finishing techniques you will need to complete the projects.

SEAMS

Whether you are joining two tiny square patches or the front and back of a pillowcase, the basic seaming method is the same. On larger panels you may be asked to neaten the edges with a zigzag or overlock stitch. Pin the two pieces with right sides facing and the raw edges and corners aligned. You can then tack larger panels if you wish, by joining with a row of long running stitches, removing the pins as you go.

STRAIGHT SEAM

Machine stitch along the specified seam allowance, using the side of the foot or the lines on the flat bed to gauge the distance between the needle and the edge. Press the seam allowance open, as shown, or press both sides to the left or right according to the instructions. This is particularly important when joining patches. Working a few stitches in the opposite direction at each end reinforces the seam.

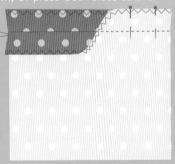

CORNER SEAM

When you come to a corner, keep the needle in the down position and lift the presser foot. Pivot the fabric and sew along the next edge. Trim the allowance to within 3mm of the stitches, then turn right side out and ease the corner into shape with a blunt pencil.

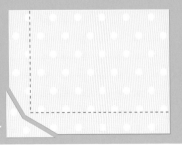

CURVED SEAM

There's only one curved seam used in all the projects, but as it's on Stanley's ear it's an important one! On an outside curve you need to reduce the amount of fabric in the allowance so that the seam will lie flat. Do this by snipping a series of evenly spaced little notches to within 2mm of the stitching, all round the curve.

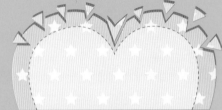

CLOSING A GAP

When making a stuffed toy or the pincushion you'll need to leave a gap in a seam through which to add the filling. Press back the allowance on each side beforeturning through, add the filling, thenpin the two edges together and slip stitch, passing the needle through the folds for a neat finish.

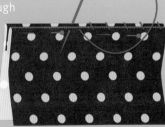

HEMS

A raw edge can be finished by folding it over and stitching down the turning, as around the top of the Dresden Plate Tote Bag on pages 66–69, or by covering it with a narrow length of bias binding for a more decorative look, which I did for the Circles Laundry Bag on pages 58–61.

SINGLE HEM

Neaten the edge of the fabric, if directed, then with the wrong side facing, fold the edge back to the required depth. Sometimes all you'll need to do at this stage is press it down, or you may have to machine stitch, just below the zigzag.

MITRED CORNER

When two single hems meet at a corner, as they do on the Tea Towel Tablecloth on pages 118–119, you need to fold them into a mitre. Press down both hems, then unfold. Turn in the corner at 45 degrees so that the creases match up to make a square and press. Trim off the corner to within 5mm of the diagonal crease, then refold and stitch down.

DOUBLE HEM

Fold and press the first turning to the given measurement, then make the second turning which may be the same or slightly deeper. Pin and tack, then machine stitch close to the inner fold or slip stitch by hand.

BOUND HEM

I bound the top edge of the Circles Laundry Bag on pages 58–61 by hand to match the appliqué stitching but mainly because it's less complicated! Lightly press the binding in half and slot it over the first edge, tacking it down as you go. When you reach a corner, fold it around the next edge, mitring the surplus at a 45 degree angle.

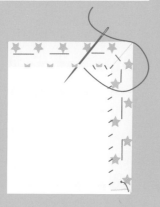

Sew down with small stitches in matching thread, stabbing the needle from side to side to catch down both folded edges at the same time.

HANDLES

This method for making fabric handles could be used instead of webbing for the Tweed Messenger Bag on pages 38–41 and the Sugarbag Doorstop on pages 120–123.

TOP STITCHED HANDLE

Cut a fabric strip twice the finished width, plus 2cm. Press under a 1cm turning along each long edge, then press in half. Tack edges together and machine stitch 3mm from the edge.

REINFORCING STITCHING

When a handle is sewn to a bag the join has to be reinforced, so that it can bear weight. Tack one end of the handle (slightly more than its width), behind the bag. Starting at the top right corner, sew a square or rectangle of machine stitches over the top. Now sew diagonally across to bottom left, back along the bottom edge and up to the top left corner.

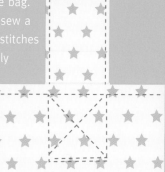

Traditional Techniques

Even if it's just replacing a lost button, sewing by hand is so enjoyable! English Patchwork was the first 'proper' sewing technique that I learnt, and I will always remember the process of joining together scraps of fabrics to make something new. There are four other classic hand techniques which have been adapted for the projects in this book.

ENGLISH PATCHWORK

Also known as Paper or Mosaic Patchwork, this centuries-old method is used primarily to piece accurate geometric shapes. The iconic hexagon quilt, so popular in the 1970s, is made in this way. Each patch is tacked over a paper template and the folded edges then sewn together. The aim at one time was to work eight or nine stitches per centimetre but we are all a little more forgiving today! A traditional way of preventing the thread from fraying as it passes repeatedly through the fabric is to draw it firmly over a block of pure beeswax.

CRAZY PATCHWORK

The Victorians invented this extravagant patchwork style, indulging their love of ornament and decoration to the full. They made fantastic confections of brocade, velvet and satin in deep colours and with rich textures, then encrusted them still further with intricate embroidery stitches. It's a combination of appliqué and patchwork, in which fragments of cloth are laid out on a plain background and fitted together like a jigsaw to create a fragmented, crazed surface. The fabric is then stitched down and the seams embellished. I've reinterpreted this technique in a fresher, lighter way with my Crazy Patchwork Cushion on pages 80–83 and for the vase that forms the basis of the Flower Picture on pages 136–139.

CATHEDRAL WINDOW

A relatively recent development, dating from the 1920s, the 'windows' are usually worked with a frame of white cotton and patterned diamond-shaped 'panes'. For the Boudoir Cushion on pages 76–79 I chose a vintage cream sateen as the background for a collection of pastel lingerie silk. Like the Suffolk Puff, this is a technique that's always explored further by innovative stitchers, and it works well with a darker background. There is a variation called Secret Garden, where an extra layer of fabric is placed within the folded square, just before the points are stitched down. This is revealed when the edges are turned back and adds extra colour to the inside of the petals.

SUFFOLK PUFFS

You won't fail to notice that this is my favourite technique at the moment and, as you'll see, I've actually managed to incorporate puffs into five of the projects. In the following pages they are used to make a cushion cover, to embellish a cardigan and to create a necklace... see if you can spot the other two. Sometimes called yo-yos or pom-poms, they are undergoing something of a revival at the moment. They are very versatile and quick to make. All you have to do is cut out a circle of fabric, sew down a turning all around the edge and draw up your thread to gather up the fabric. To speed up this process you can even buy clever little gadgets that help you create puffs in a range of different sizes.

HAND APPLIQUÉ

Folded edge appliqué is another technique with a long history. It involves cutting out fabric shapes, tacking a narrow hem around the edge, then sewing the patch to a background. In mid-nineteenth century America it was used to create wonderfully colourful and ornate quilts, especially around the seaport of Baltimore. Folding narrow hems can prove fiddly, so for the Circles Laundry Bag shown opposite and the Dresden Plate Tote Bag and Cushion on pages 66–71, you'll learn you how to tack the fabric over a template first to create perfect curves.

Hand Appliqué

This term derives directly from the French verb 'appliquer' which translates as 'to put on', consequently the technique involves cutting out small pieces of fabric and literally putting them on to a background. The traditional way of doing this by hand is explained on the previous page, but you can also attach the shapes with iron-on fusible bonding web – a much quicker method. This type of appliqué was explored in my first sewing book *Make!*, where it was used to recreate designs from some of my most popular fabrics. This time simpler shapes and motifs are used as patches, to add decoration to bags, garments and cushions.

BONDING WEB

Fusible bonding web is a sheet of translucent paper with a backing of heat-activated adhesive. There are several types and weights sold under different trade names, but they are all do the same thing. Ensure you buy the correct one for your appliqué fabric: if you use heavyweight web on silk or lawn the adhesive will show through the fine weave.

All you have to do is trace the reversed outline of the motif directly on to the paper side of the web. Cut it out roughly and with the adhesive side downwards, iron the paper to the wrong side of the appliqué fabric (following the manufacturer's guidelines). Now trim precisely around the pencil line. Peel away the paper, place the motif on the background in its final position, and press with a hot iron to fuse the adhesive. Broderie Perse shapes (see below) can also be fixed down with bonding web. Cut a piece that is slightly larger than your chosen part of the fabric, iron it to the wrong side, then cut around the printed outline.

EDGING YOUR MOTIFS

Your motifs are now in place but the edges are still raw, so you'll need to neaten them to stop them fraying. The functional way to do this is by machine, with a narrow, closely-spaced zigzag or with one of the more decorative stitches. Use a matching thread if you want an invisible border (like that on the Hounds Bag on pages 54–57). A hand-embroidered finish would always be my first choice however, and on pages 28 and 29 you'll find instructions for some of my favourite stitches.

BRODERIE PERSE

If you've ever snipped out images from a magazine and glued them into a scrapbook (a rainy-day pastime for most kids at some stage), you'll be familiar with the idea behind Broderie Perse. This is another French term, meaning Persian Embroidery, although it's not from Persia and it isn't really embroidery! The earliest surviving examples date from the 1600s when exotic floral chintz was first imported into England by the East India Company. Individual flowers, leaves, birds and butterflies were cut from this highly-prized fabric and then sewn on to a plain background to form new pictorial designs.

Any printed fabric can be used for Broderie Perse and you can really let your imagination run riot when it comes to collaging the motifs. I found some fabulous full-blown roses on a furnishing remnant to fill the vase in the Flower Picture, shown at almost full-size on pages 138–139. This project also incorporates vintage buttons and some hand embroidery to draw in the stems and embellish the flowers. A more random interpretation can be found on the linen Appliqué Tea Towel in the country kitchen on pages 128–129. These nostalgic designs came from a length of homemaker-style barkcloth curtaining and are edged with an unobtrusive buttonhole stitch, worked in thread to match the fabric background. The third Broderie Perse project is the Hounds Bag on pages 54–57, which recycles motifs from a much more delicate fabric – a twill silk headscarf.

Embroidery & Embellishments

Both patchwork and appliqué are so decorative in themselves that they scarcely need any more surface decoration, but sometimes an extra detail can provide the finishing touch that makes a piece really stand out. Embellishment can be understated – a line of simple stitches around a tweed patch for example – or an integral part of the overall design, like the feather stitch around the patches on the Crazy Patch Cushion.

BUTTONS

Buttons of all shapes and sizes can be used for practical purposes – fastening a pillowcase or securing a bag handle – or as pure ornament. I picked out a varied selection from my tin of vintage buttons to add highlights of colour and texture to the Flower Picture on pages 138–141. Keep an eye out for old cloth laundry buttons and those made from early plastics, wood or pressed glass. Mother-of-pearl buttons have a neutral, natural finish that goes well with any fabric and you can add extra colour by sewing them on with bright embroidery thread.

However carefully you stitch, there may be times when your seams don't line up perfectly at the corners. Joins that are not quite precise can be concealed with the careful placing of a few buttons… this secret cheat worked especially well on the Boudoir Cushion and it's also good for misaligned square patches.

LACE, RIBBON AND CORD

I'm not usually keen on a lot of frilly lace, but used with discretion it can be very effective. The centre panel of the Rose Knitting Bag on pages 50–53 is frramed with a simple triangular edging, which proved the perfect counterpoint to the white rose and daisy print. In the same way the fine pink piping around the Crazy Patch Cushion on pages 80–83 picks up the colour of the embroidery thread and outlines the patchwork square.

If you don't fancy making your own piping and setting it into the seam you can simply sew a length cord or other trimming around the edge of the finished cushion. Shiny or cotton cord also makes an attractive drawstring for large and small bags, and you can finish off the ends with a few beads or a fabric tab. Ricrac is a good alternative to lace, and can be used as a border or inserted in seams to give a discreet scalloped finish. Children's garments are an exception to minimalism and a ribbon bow gives character to the Bunny Sweater on pages 140–141.

STITCHERY

You can create some interesting embellishments with just a few hand embroidery stitches, all of which are shown on the next two pages. Edge appliqué patches with blanket or coral stitch and cover plain seams with feather and fly stitches. Personalise your projects with a monogram worked in back or chain stitch. I have just discovered figural red work embroidery which I chose for the embroidered Red Hens Bag on pages 42–45.

There are several ways to transfer the hen or any other photocopied outline on to fabric. The simplest is to use dressmaker's carbon paper. Sandwich together the fabric, the face-down carbon, then the photocopy, taping down each layer so they don't shift. Draw firmly over the outline with a ballpoint pen. Alternatively you can improvise a light box. Masking tape the outline to a bright window, tape the fabric to the paper and trace the outline with a sharp pencil.

Embroidery Stitches

All the stitching in this book is worked with a long-eyed needle and stranded embroidery cotton or tapestry yarn. Both threads come in a skein that is held together with one wide and one narrow paper band. Hold on to the narrow band and pull the loose end of the thread gently to withdraw it, then cut off a 45cm length. Stranded embroidery cotton is made up of six loosely twisted threads, which can easily be separated. Working with all six strands gives bold stitches and three a medium line whilst two create a much finer effect. The project steps will always tell you how many to use.

RUNNING STITCH

This basic stitch is used in English patchwork for tacking fabric to templates and on a smaller scale, for quilting. It provides the simple outline around each square on the Tweed Messenger Bag on pages 38–41. The stitches should all be the same length, as should the spaces between them.

BACK STITCH

I used this for the wool CK cipher on the Tweed Messenger Bag on pages 38–41 and to 'draw' the red work hens on the embroidered Red Hens Bag on pages 42–45. Bring the needle up one stitch length from the beginning of the line, then take it back to the start point. Come up again one stitch length ahead of this first stitch and continue, keeping the stitches regular.

STRAIGHT STITCH

Tiny upright or angled straight stitches can be used to anchor appliqué patches or to add details, like the Blanket Bunny's whiskers on pages 104–105. Simply come up at A and down again at B to make a short straight line.

SATIN STITCH

So called because of its smooth, shiny finish, this is consists of a series of straight stitches worked alongside each other in the same direction, from A to B. Vary the lengths to fill the shape being worked.

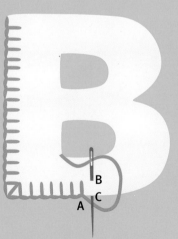

BLANKET STITCH

This classic edging stitch appears on the Appliqué Tea Towel on pages 128–29 where it was used to neaten the edge of the motifs. Come up at A, then take the needle up to B, through the fabric and out directly below at C. Loop the thread under the needle and pull it through. Repeat this sequence to the end.

TAILOR'S BUTTONHOLE STITCH

A reinforced version of blanket stitch, this was used on the Bunny Sweater on pages 142–143. Starting at A, take the needle down at B, in front of the thread and bring the point through at C. Loop the thread from left to right and pull through, lifting the needle so that the thread forms a small knot at the edge of the motif.

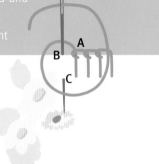

CHAIN STITCH

Use this for flexible wide outlines like the stems on the Flower Picture on pages 138–139 and for monograms or other lettering. Bring the needle out at A, then reinsert it the same place. Bring the point out at B and loop the thread from left to right under the needle. Hold the loop down and pull the needle through gently to draw up the thread. Finish off with straight stitch over the last loop.

LAZY DAISY STITCH

Single chain stitches make good petals but I worked a few long thin ones to make the tuft at the top of the Blanket Bunny's carrot! Work as for chain stitch, anchoring each loop with a short straight stitch.

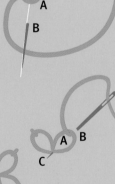

SINGLE FEATER STITCH

This variation on blanket stitch appears on the Flower Picture on pages 138–139 where it's used to edge the circular patches. Come up at A and insert the needle at B. Bring the point out at C, below B and in line with A. Loop the thread under the needle and pull through.

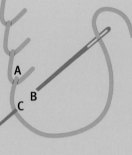

FEATHER STITCH

Look out for this pretty stitch on the embroidered Crazy Patch Cushion on pages 80–83 and the Red Hens Bag on pages 42–45. Keep all the stitches the same length and at the same angle on either side for a neat appearance. Come up at A and take it down at B forming a loose stitch. Bring the point out at C, over the thread and pull through. Work the next angled stitch from D to E over the looped thread. Repeat these two stitches to the end.

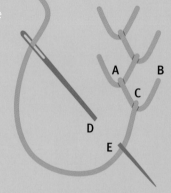

FLY STITCH

This is another good stitch to work over seams and I used it as an alternative to feather stitch on the Flower Picture vase on pages 138–139. Come up at A and take the needle back down at B, then back up at an angle, at C. Pull through over the thread and go down again, directly below at D. Repeat this stitch to form a continuous row.

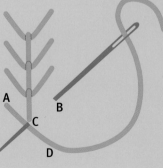

Choosing Fabrics

When it comes to selecting fabrics for patchwork and appliqué, you'll find the choice is limitless! Specialist quilt shops and department stores are piled high with rolls of new cloth and are a good source of remnants and fat quarters (the quilter's term for a 55 x 50cm rectangle). Don't forget, however, to search charity shops, flea markets and even the back of your own wardrobe for old fabrics to recycle in true patchwork tradition. For the items in this book I've used everything from silk scarves and tablecloths to hand-woven tweed and antique curtain material. The following guidelines will help you pick the right fabric for your own projects.

VINTAGE TEXTILES

Almost any vintage fabric can be used to make patchwork, as long as it is in good condition. Check carefully for stains, rust-marks or signs of wear cut away these areas. Holding the fabric up to the light will enable you to see where the threads have worn thin. Even if it appears to be in good condition, I always like to launder old cotton or linen first – the fabric often needs freshening up and if it can stand up to a gentle machine wash, it will be strong enough to sew.

COTTON AND LINEN

There is a wealth of wonderful domestic linen out there that's just waiting for you to come along: look out for hand-embroidered napkins, runners, pillowcases and dressing table mats. Fine quality sheets make good backings for projects like the Circles Laundry Bag on pages 58–61 or the Star Throw on pages 106–109 and even humble stripey tea towels come into their own when patched together to make a tablecloth. Printed versions are a good alternative to buying wider and more expensive fabrics – I was especially pleased with the Floral and Spot Tote Bag on pages 34–37, which is made from co-ordinating floral and spotty tea towels.

SILKS AND WOOLLENS

The rich textures of velvet, satin and silk add another dimension to patchwork, but these fabrics aren't always easy to work with. Delicate silk patches need to be backed with interfacing to hold their shape – as with the colourful Harlequin Bag on pages 46–49 – or combined with firmer fabrics. The 'Cathedral Window' technique used for the Boudoir Cushion on pages 76–79 is a good example of how to do this. Projects like floor cushions, that will get a lot of hard use, need to be made from larger patches of thicker materials, so old blankets are ideal for these (especially if you've had moths in the house).

PRINTS AND PATTERNS

Small-scale floral dress fabrics are the classic choice for patchwork, and work best when a few plain colours are thrown into the blend. You can mix large and small prints with checks and ginghams, but try to keep within a limited colour palette as I did for the Child's Cushion on pages 92–95, or the overall effect can be a bit overwhelming. I particularly like working with printed or woven stripes, cutting them into square or rectangular patches, then reassembling them to make new geometric patterns. At first glance, you wouldn't think that all the fabric for Personalised Dog Bed on pages 132–135 was salvaged from a single blanket.

'Fussy cut' patches of patterned fabrics, like those I made for the Hexagon Pincushion on pages 130–131, create rhythmic repeating designs or you can select interesting individual motifs for appliqué patches – I couldn't resist the nostalgic racing cars used on the Patched Dungarees on pages 142–143. For the framed Flower Picture on pages 138–141 I cut out a series of large rose motifs from glazed chintz and stitched them to a length of plain damask – an old technique called Broderie Perse first used when new fabrics were scarce and costly.

Patch! Projects

Designing the projects for this book, selecting the perfect fabrics and deciding exactly which techniques to use, was a hugely enjoyable task. Whether you're a needlework novice or an experienced stitcher, I hope you'll enjoy them as much as I have done.

Floral & Spot Tote Bag

MATERIALS
140 x 70cm spot print fabric
140 x 40cm floral print fabric
stranded embroidery thread in red
matching sewing thread
sewing machine
sewing kit

CUTTING OUT
from spot print fabric
seventeen 12cm squares
two 52 x 32cm lining panels
one 42 x 12cm lining base
from floral print fabric
seventeen 12cm squares
one 22 x 12cm pocket
two 60 x 8cm handle strips

SKILL LEVEL: 2

Here's a relaxed and roomy bag that's just the right size for a quick trip to your local shop, or for carrying books and a laptop. It's made from one of my all-time favourite fabric combinations – spots and flowers – and I love the contrast in scale between the bold denim-look polka dots and the delicate sprays of briar roses on their dark indigo background.

The seam allowance throughout is 1cm.

1 Lay out the thirty squares that make up the main bag in a chequerboard pattern, in three horizontal rows of ten. Sew them together in vertical rows of three, with right sides facing. You'll find detailed instructions for this in the Patch! Basics section, on page 20.

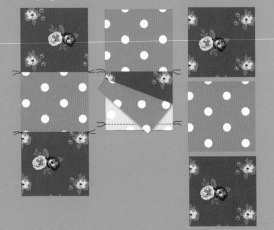

2 Press the seam allowances in opposite directions so that they will lie flat when the rows are joined. For each row with a spot square at the top and bottom, press the seams downwards and for each row with a floral square at the top and bottom, press the seams upwards.

3 Join the rows together to make a long rectangle. With right sides facing, match the long edges so that the seams butt up against each other. Insert a pin at each seam line and at the top and bottom corners, then machine stitch.

4 Press all the vertical seams open. Seam and press the two side edges to make a cylinder of patchwork. Press.

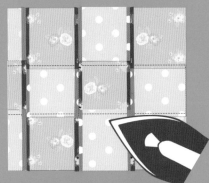

5 Sew the remaining four squares together to make the base, alternating the spot and floral prints. Press the seams open.

top tip I'LL LET YOU INTO A SECRET... THIS BAG IS ACTUALLY MADE FROM FOUR COTTON TEA TOWELS, ALWAYS A GREAT SOURCE OF NEW FABRIC IN SMALLER QUANTITIES!

Floral & Spot Tote Bag

6 With right sides facing inwards, pin one long edge of the bag base to four squares along the bottom edge of the main bag, matching the open seams. Pin the other long edge to the opposite side of the bag, leaving the short edges open. Make a 5mm snip into the bottom of each corner seam to open out the allowance. Machine stitch these two seams, starting and finishing each line of stitching 1cm from the short edge and working a few backwards stitches to strengthen.

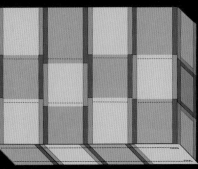

7 Pin the short edges of the base to the bag and machine stitch. Work two more rounds of stitching first lines to reinforce the seam.

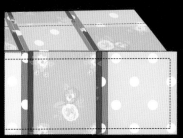

8 Using a thick crewel needle and three strands of red embroidery thread, work a line of running stitch, 5mm in from each side seam.

9 Neaten the top edge of the pocket with a narrow double hem. Press under a 1cm turning along the other three sides. Pin the pocket to one lining panel, 6cm down from the top edge and 11cm in from the left side edge. Machine down in place, working a few extra stitches at the beginning and end of the seam.

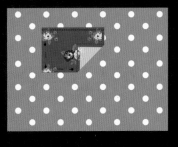

10 With right sides facing, join the two edges of the lining panels to make a cylinder. Press the seams open, then press back a 15mm turning around the top edge. Make a 6mm snip into the seam allowance on the bag at each corner as for the main bag. With right sides facing, pin on the lining base, lining up two opposite corners to the two seams. Sew in place with two rounds of stitching.

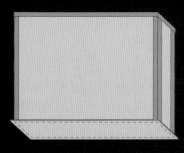

11 Slip the lining inside the bag, matching up the base and two side edge seams. Pin together around the opening – the lining should sit about 5mm down from the top edge of the bag. Machine stitch 3mm from the top edge of the lining.

12 Press each handle strip in half widthways and unfold. Press a 1cm turning each of the four edges, then re-press the centre crease. Machine stitch 3mm from each long edge. Tack the ends of the handles to the sides of the bag so that they lie 5cm down from the top edge and overlap the side patchwork seams. Sew down with rectangles of reinforcing stitch (see page 21).

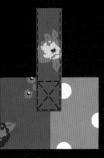

top tip LINES OF TOP STITCHING ALONG EACH SIDE SEAM DEFINE THE SHAPE OF THE BAG. TO MAKE THEM STAND OUT, MATCH THE COLOUR OF THE THREAD TO THE FABRIC: I CHOSE A WARM RED THAT HIGHLIGHTS THE ROSE DETAIL.

Tweed Messenger Bag

MATERIALS

eighteen 14cm squares tweed fabric
tapestry yarn in shades to match
large crewel needle
75 x 38cm cotton fabric for lining
125cm of 5cm-wide webbing for
  bag handle
matching sewing thread
quilter's ruler
chalk pencil
sewing machine
sewing kit

SKILL LEVEL: 1

Both practical and roomy, there's plenty of space in this over-shoulder messenger bag for all your daily essentials. It's quick to make from simple squares of tweed. I used a mixture of both old and new fabrics, and the soft, natural colours of the wool blend together really well. Each patch is outlined with a round of running stitches worked in tapestry yarn and the one in the centre is monogrammed.

1 Using a quilter's ruler and chalk pencil, mark a guideline on each tweed square, 2cm in from the edge. Thread the crewel needle with tapestry yarn to match each colour in turn, and sew a line of small running stitches around every chalk outline.

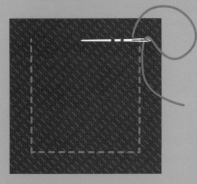

2 Arrange the first nine squares in three horizontal rows of three, moving them about until you have a balanced arrangement of colour and pattern.

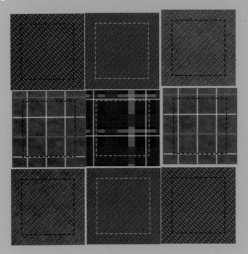

3 Draw your initials on the centre square using the chalk pencil. Embroider over the lines with small back stitches (see page 30).

4 Join the squares in horizontal rows, starting at the bottom left corner. Pin the right edge of the first square to the left edge of the second square and machine stitch with a 12mm seam allowance. Pin and sew the third square in the same way. Press the two seams towards the left.

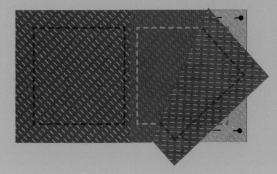

top tip I MADE MY BAG WITH A PATCHWORK PANEL AT BOTH FRONT AND BACK, BUT YOU COULD USE A SINGLE LARGE SQUARE OF TWEED TO MAKE A PLAIN REVERSE SIDE. A SMALL MONOGRAM IN THE CORNER WOULD PROVIDE EXTRA VISUAL INTEREST.

Tweed Messenger Bag

5 Join the three centre squares and press the seams to the right, then sew the top three squares together and press the seam towards the left.

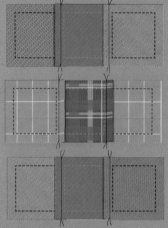

6 With right sides facing, pin the bottom edge of the top row to the top edge of the centre row so that the seams match up. Insert a pin at both points where the seams meet and at each corner. Machine stitch 12mm leaving a 12mm allowance. Add the bottom row in the same way and press all the horizontal seams upwards.

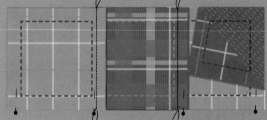

7 Sew the nine remaining squares together in the same way to make the back of the bag. Press the horizontal seams downwards. Pin the side and bottom edges of the front and back together with right sides facing, once again matching the corners and seams.

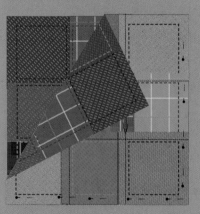

8 Machine stitch 12mm from the edge, then stitch over the line once again to reinforce. Clip a small triangle from each bottom corner so that they will lie flat (see page **). Turn the bag right side out, ease out the corners and press lightly.

9 Neaten the top edge by turning back and tacking down a 12mm turning. You will need to open out the seams as you go, so that the opening doesn't become too lumpy.

10 Pin the ends of the handle to the inside top corners of the bag, overlapping them by 5cm. The seams should lie halfway across the webbing. Tack in place, then machine stitch a rectangle of reinforcing stitches (see page **).

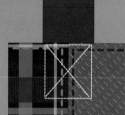

11 Fold the lining in half with right sides facing. Pin and machine stitch the two side edges with a 1cm seam, then press back a 3cm turning all around the opening. Slip the lining inside the bag, matching up the side seams. Pin the folded edge 5mm below the top of the bag, then slip stitch it in place.

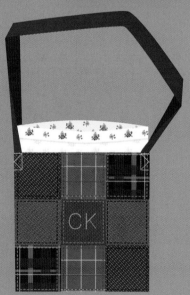

top tip IF YOU CAN'T FIND COTTON WEBBING IN THE RIGHT WIDTH OR SHADE, STITCH YOUR OWN WOOLLEN HANDLE FROM A 125 x 12CM LENGTH OF TWEED, FOLLOWING THE INSTRUCTIONS FOR MAKING STRAPS ON PAGE 21.

Red Hens Bag

MATERIALS

1m x 50cm red cotton fabric
50 x 15cm white linen fabric
1m x 50cm striped cotton fabric
2m of 2.5cm-wide white bias binding
off-white and red stranded cotton
   embroidery thread
four 2.5cm buttons
matching sewing thread
sewing machine
sewing kit

CUTTING OUT

from red cotton fabric
two 10 x 41cm side gussets
one 10 x 38cm bottom gusset
one 38 x 41cm back panel
two 8 x 70cm straps
two 8 x 15cm tabs
from striped cotton fabric
two 38 x 41cm side panels
two 10 x 41cm side gussets
one 10 x 38cm bottom gusset

SKILL LEVEL: 3

Redwork embroidery – simple outline drawings stitched on to a plain white background – was hugely popular at the turn of the nineteenth century. Over a hundred years on, it's undergoing a well-deserved revival. The finished embroideries in this distinctive red have long been combined with crimson cloth to make striking, graphic patchwork. I've started with this simple country-style bag... but dream of making a whole quilt, with an entire flock of little red hens and roosters.

The seam allowance throughout is 1cm.

1 Using the full-sized template on page 156, trace two left-facing and two right-facing hens within their rectangles on to the white linen fabric (see how to do this on page 26). Leave at least 6cm between each image. Stitch over the hen outlines in small back stitches, using three strands of thread, and embroider the frames in feather stitch (see pages 30 and 31).

2 Trace the rectangle five times on to the red cotton fabric and work a round of off-white feather stitch around each outline, again with three strands of thread.

3 Trim each completed patch down to 14 x 15cm, making sure that there is an equal margin around the feather stitching.

4 Arrange the patches in three rows of three, alternating red and white, and with all the chickens facing inwards. With right sides facing, pin the side edges of the first two together and machine stitch.

5 Add the third patch to the other side of the chicken, then join the other two rows. Press all the seams towards the red patches.

top tip FOR A FIXED, RATHER THAN AN ADJUSTABLE, HANDLE MAKE THE STRAP 10CM LONGER AND SEW

THE ENDS TO THE SIDE GUSSETS OF THE BAG. YOU COULD ALWAYS ADD THE BUTTONS AS A DECORATIVE FEATURE.

Red Hens Bag

6 Pin the bottom edge of the top row and the top edge of the centre row together, with right sides facing, so that the seam allowances all butt up against each other. Insert the pins along the seam lines and at both corners. Machine stitch. Add the bottom row in the same way. Press the seams open.

7 Pin the short ends of the side gussets to the bottom gusset to make a long strip, with right sides facing. Machine stitch, starting and finishing 1cm from the end of each seam line.

8 With right sides together, pin one long edge of the completed gusset strip to the side and bottom edges of the back panel. Open out the unstitched ends of the seams so that the gusset fits neatly around the bottom corners. Tack in place then machine stitch, working an extra row at each corner to reinforce. Add the front panel in the same way, then turn the bag right side out and press the seams lightly. Press under a 1cm turning around the opening.

9 Make up the striped lining in exactly the same way as the bag, but don't turn it through. Press back a 1cm turning around the top edge.

10 Trim one end of each of the four strap and tabs into a shallow curve. Press under a 1cm turning around each piece. Press the bias binding in half width ways.

11 Tack the binding to the wrong side of the long and curved edges of one strap and one tab so 5mm overlaps to the right side. Tack the second strap and tab in place so the binding is sandwiched between them and machine stitch 3mm from the edge. Make two buttonholes, by hand or machine, 5mm and 10mm from the end of the strap. They should lie parallel to the long edges.

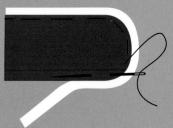

12 Pin and tack the completed strap to the left side gusset, so that 3cm lies inside the main bag. Attach the tab to the right side in the same way, then slip in the lining. Match up the seams and pin them together so that the top edge of the lining lies 5mm below the opening. Hand stitch the two together, making sure that the needle goes through the turned back hem around the main bag only, and the stitches don't show on the right side. Work extra stitches along the base of the strap and tab, or sew a rectangle of machine reinforcing stitches (see page 21) at the top of each side gusset.

13 Finish off by sewing two of the buttons to the tab 5cm apart, and the other pair to the side gusset, also 5cm apart.

top tip ADAPT THIS IDEA TO MAKE AN AUTOGRAPH BAG AS AN END-OF-TERM SOUVENIR: GET YOUR BEST FRIENDS TO SIGN FEATHER-STITCH TRIMMED PATCHES AND BACK STITCH OVER THEIR WRITING.

Harlequin Bag

MATERIALS

remnants of velvet and silk fabrics
   in a range of colours
lightweight iron-on interfacing
1.5m of 5mm cord
65 x 25cm toning velvet fabric
15cm circle of medium-weight card
matching sewing thread
glue stick
sewing machine
scrap paper

CUTTING OUT

from toning velvet fabric
two 15cm circles for bag and
   lining base
38 x 23cm rectangle for lining

SKILL LEVEL: 3

When I came across a collection of vivid antique silk and velvet scraps I was intrigued by the way the jewel-like colours – which range from ruby and topaz through to jade and amethyst – worked together, in true Harlequin style. I wanted to make them into something very special, and so came up with this velvet-lined drawstring bag design. It is made up of tiny diamond patches, hand-stitched over foundation papers… the perfect place to store your most treasured possessions.

1 Following the manufacturer's instructions, strengthen the finest silk fabrics by fusing lightweight iron-on interfacing to the wrong side.

2 You will need 139 diamond patches, 135 for the bag and four for the drawstring tabs. Cut out the backing papers using the template on page 156 as your guide and cover each one with fabric, mitring the corners neatly. You'll find detailed instructions for this on page 23.

3 Sew the patches together in fifteen diagonal rows of nine diamonds.

4 Join the completed rows to make a long rectangle.

5 With right sides facing, sew the two short edges of the rectangle together to make a cylinder.

6 Press lightly from the wrong side, then unpick all the tacking papers. Fold back and tack down the top halves of the diamonds at the top and bottom to give a straight edge around each opening.

top tip YOU CAN JOIN THE DIAMONDS RANDOMLY, OR LAY THEM ALL OUT FIRST, IN FIFTEEN DIAGONAL ROWS OF NINE AND SHUFFLE THEM AROUND TO CREATE A MORE BALANCED ARRANGEMENT.

Harlequin Bag

7 Divide the bottom edge into four equal sections by inserting four pins into the fold, with three and a half patches between them. This will help you gather the edge evenly when you sew on the base.

8 Prepare the base by ruling two lines across the cardboard circle, dividing it into quarter sections. Sew a line of long running stitches 5mm from the edge of one velvet circle. Coat the back of the card lightly with a glue stick and place it centrally on the wrong side of the velvet. Gather up the thread so that the edge covers the card and fasten off securely. Insert four pins into the card, one at the end of each line.

9 Sew a line of running stitch 5mm from the bottom edge of the bag and draw it up until the opening is 1cm smaller in diameter than the velvet base. Line up the marker pins and pin the base centrally to the gathered opening – this is rather an awkward process, so you need to 'stab' the pins through the edge of the velvet and into the patchwork. Slip stitch the base to the bag with matching thread.

10 With right sides facing, pin the two short edges of the velvet rectangle together and join with a 1cm seam. Press back a 1cm turning around the top edge. Pin eight pins around the bottom edge at 4.5cm intervals.

11 Fold the remaining velvet circle in half, then quarters and position a pin at each fold. Now add another pin between each pair, to divide the circumference in eight equal section. With right sides facing, tack the base to the bag, matching the pins. Machine stitch 1cm from the edge and trim the seam allowance back to 3mm.

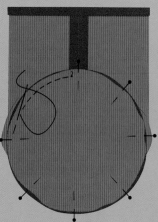

12 Sit the lining inside the bag and pin the two top edges together so that they line up exactly. Join together by hand, with a round of slip stitch.

13 To make the drawstring channel, machine two parallel rounds of straight stitch around the opening, 2.5 and 5cm down from the top edge. Unpick one of the diagonal lines of hand stitching between these two rows and secure the other ends of the seams with a few extra stitches. Make the other opening directly opposite, in the same way.

14 Cut the cord in half and secure one end to an elastic threader or small safety pin. Feed it through one opening, all the way around the drawstring channel, then back out of the opening. Thread the remaining half through the other opening.

15 Tie both cords together in an overhand knot, about 10m from the ends. Trim to 6cm. Fold one of the last diamonds in half lengthways and hold it over one cord so that the raw end is completely enclosed. Slip stitch the edges together, stab stitching through the cord. Unpick the tacking. Do the same on the other three ends.

top tip CHECK ANTIQUE FABRICS FOR ANY DAMAGED AREAS THAT MIGHT NOT BE STRONG ENOUGH FOR RE-USE. IF YOU HOLD THEM UP TO THE LIGHT YOU CAN EASILY DETECT ANY WORN PATCHES.

Rose Knitting Bag

MATERIALS

60 x 25cm red floral print fabric
120 x 50cm green spot print fabric
1m narrow lace
pair of bag handles
matching sewing thread
pencil and ruler
sewing machine
sewing kit

CUTTING OUT

from red floral print fabric
one 27 x 15cm centre flower panel
ten 7cm squares
from green spot print fabric
twelve 7cm squares
three 37 x 27cm side panels
two 7 x 58cm gussets
four 5 x 8 handle loops

SKILL LEVEL: 2

Vintage furnishing fabrics, like the classic rose curtain I found for this cheerful knitting bag, are idea for patchwork projects. The larger scale patterns make a change from small ditsy prints and are very versatile. I chose a complete rose motif for the octagon and then picked out a few of the smaller floral sprays to make the squares. The triangular lace trimming frames the centre panel perfectly, echoing the shape and colour of the petals.

The seam allowance throughout is 1cm.

1 Start off by joining the squares. With right sides facing, sew four spot and three floral patches together for the top and bottom strips, alternating the fabrics. Sew two floral patches to two spot squares for the side strips. Press all the seam allowances towards the floral squares.

2 Using a sharp pencil and a ruler, draw a diagonal line across the wrong side of the remaining four spot squares. Pin one to each corner of the flower panel with the line running from edge to edge. Machine stitch along the pencil lines, then trim the surplus fabric leaving a 1cm allowance on each seam. Press all the seams towards the centre panel.

3 Slip stitch the lace around the edge of the flower panel. Neaten the end by trimming it to 6mm, folding it back and stitching down.

4 With right sides facing, pin and stitch the two three-patch side strips to the side edges of the centre panel. Press the seams towards the centre. Pin on the top and bottom strips, matching the seams and corners. Machine stitch, then press the seams inwards.

top tip IF YOU ARE USING A PIECE OF OLD FABRIC, HOLD IT UP TO THE LIGHT TO CHECK FOR SMALL HOLES OR ANY PARTS THAT HAVE WORN TOO THIN FOR USE. MARK THESE WITH STICKY LABELS AND CUT YOUR PATCHES FROM THE SOUND AREAS.

Rose
Knitting Bag

5 Draw a diagonal line across each bottom corner square and cut across these marks. Pin the finished front panel to one of the green spot side panels and snip a triangle from each bottom corner so that the two are the same size. Do the same with the other two side panels. Mark the 1cm seam allowance along the side and bottom edges of all four panels.

6 With right sides facing, pin one of the gusset strips to the side edge of a green spot panel. Machine stitch along the pencil line, as far as the corner. Sew a few reverse stitches to secure the end of the seam. Snip off the thread and remove the fabric from the machine. Make an 8mm snip into the seam allowance of the gusset, in line with the end of the seam.

7 Now swivel the gusset round so that the edge lies along the diagonal corner and pin the two layers together. Carry on machine stitching along the line, just as far as the next angle. Snip the allowance again, then sew the bottom edge and the second corner in the same way. Trim the end of the gusset in line with the top edge of the bag.

8 Sew on the front panel to complete the main bag. Turn right side out, ease out the corners and press the seams lightly. Press under and tack down a 1cm turning around the opening.

9 Press under a 1cm turning along each long edge of the four handle loops. Thread them through the holes in the handles, lining up the bottom edges.

10 Position a handle so that it lies centrally along the bag front. Pin, then tack the bottom edges of the handle loops to the wrong side of the opening, so that 2cm projects above the top edge. Tack the other handle to the back panel in the corresponding position.

11 Make up the lining and press the opening as for the main bag, but don't turn it through. Slip the lining into the bag. Match up the side seams and the top edges precisely. Tack the two together and machine stitch around the top edge, 3mm from the opening.

top tip I REALLY LIKED THESE TRANSPARENT BAG HANDLES, WHICH ARE UNDERSTATED AND DON'T DOMINATE THE PRETTY PRINTS. INSTEAD OF INTRODUCING ANOTHER COLOUR, NATURAL BAMBOO WOULD MAKE A GOOD ALTERNATIVE IF YOU CAN'T FIND ANYTHING SIMILAR.

Hounds Bag

MATERIALS
70 x 90cm striped fabric
75 x 50cm floral print fabric for lining
old silk scarf or printed fabric
fusible bonding web
matching sewing thread
sewing machine
sewing kit

CUTTING OUT
from striped fabric
The stripes should run vertically on
each piece.
one 35 x 90cm rectangle for main bag
two 10 x 40cm side gussets
two 8 x 60cm straps
from floral print lining fabric
two 35 x 47cm rectangles

SKILL LEVEL: 2

Appliqué patches can be made from all kinds of unexpected fabrics, and I'm always on the look out for illustrative one-off prints. These four perky hounds started out on a vintage silk headscarf, of the kind worn by generations of countrywomen and dog-lovers. Such fine fabric needs reinforcement if it is to stand up to everyday wear and tear, so a fusible bonding web was used to fix them on to the deckchair striped canvas, and the raw edges were reinforced with machine stitch.

1 Decide which motifs from the patterned fabric you wish to use and plan their positions on the bag. Cut them out roughly and iron the fusible web onto the wrong side, following the manufacturer's instructions. Cut around the outlines and peel off the backing papers

2 Fold the bag in half lengthways and insert a pin at each side edge to mark the centre point.

3 Fold up the top 40cm – this will be the front of the bag. Arrange the motifs as you wish, remembering to leave at least 5cm at the top edge, then iron them in place. Work a round of 3mm wide machine blanket or zigzag stitches around the edge of each shape in matching thread.

4 Mark the centre bottom edge of the two side gussets with pins. With right sides facing, place one gusset across the bag, matching the pin to the centre point of the bag.

5 Make two 8mm snips into the seam allowance of the bag in line, 1cm in from each side edge of the gusset, so that it will fold around the corners. Pin the side edges of the bag to the sides of the gusset.

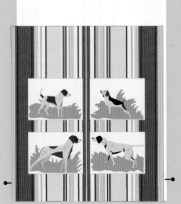

top tip YOU WILL NEED TO ALLOW MORE FABRIC TO MAKE A SYMMETRICALLY STRIPED BAG AND TO
MATCH THE SIDE GUSSETS AND STRAPS. THIS EXTRA AMOUNT WILL DEPEND ON THE WIDTH OF THE REPEAT.

54

Hounds Bag

6 Machine stitch the bag to the gusset with a 1cm seam. Work three short diagonal lines of stitching across the corners to reinforce them, then trim the seam allowance at the corner back to 4mm (see page 20). Join the other gusset in the same way.

7 Press the seams open and then press back a 3mm turning around the opening. Turn the bag right side out and ease out the corners into right angles.

8 Pin the two lining pieces together with right sides facing and machine stitch around the side and bottom edges leaving a 1cm seam allowance. Press the seams open.

9 Now make a t-junction seam at each bottom corner to give depth to the lining. Fold it so that one side seam lies along the bottom seam. Draw an 8cm line across the corner, then machine stitch along this line. Trim the seam back to 4mm. Do the same at the other corner, then press back a 3.5mm turning around the top edge.

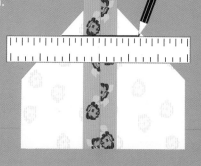

10 Slip the lining inside the bag, matching up the side seams. Pin the two together so that the lining lies 3mm below the top edge of the bag. Machine stitch 5mm from the top edge.

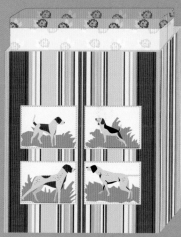

11 To make up the straps, press under a 1cm turning along each short, then each long edge of the two strips. Press them in half with wrong sides facing. Pin the folded edges together and machine stitch all round, 3mm from the edge.

12 Pin and tack the ends of the strap to the back and front of the bag and machine stitch down with a rectangle of reinforcing stitches (see page 21).

top tip ALTHOUGH YOU DON'T ALWAYS SEE THE LINING FABRIC, THAT DOESN'T MEAN IT HAS GO UNNOTICED.

I USED ONE OF MY FLORAL PRINTS INSIDE THIS BAG, IN A COLOURWAY TO MATCH THE CANVAS.

Circles Laundry Bag

MATERIALS

85 x 65cm white linen fabric
scraps of floral print fabric
2m pink bias binding
80cm pink cord
matching sewing thread
sewing kit
dressmaker's pen or chalk pencil
long ruler or 60cm quilter's rule
thin card

SKILL LEVEL: 2

This laundry bag is hand appliquéd with a geometric arrangement of petal shapes, a traditional pattern known as 'Hidden Circles'. This is a wonderful way to repurpose tiny pieces of fabric, and the more prints you can find, the more interesting the finished bag will look. I chose a random mixture from my collection of old dress-making cottons and added a few vintage American feed sack fabrics – you'll see how a wide range of floral designs always sit happily together even though they vary in scale and colour.

CUTTING OUT

from white linen fabric
one 60 x 62cm rectangle
from floral print fabric
fifty large petals, using the template on page 156 and following the outer line on the template from thin card
several small petals, following the inner line on the template

1 Prepare each of the petals for appliqué. Pin a card template centrally on the wrong side of the fabric. Turn back the hem and sew it down through the card with long running stitches. Fold the corners into neat points. Press the turning with a hot iron and when cool, unpick the thread. After a while the card templates may become distorted, so change them regularly.

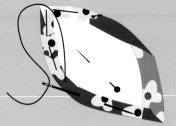

2 The petals have to be positioned accurately before they are stitched down. You can do this by eye, or by drawing a grid directly on to the fabric. Fold the fabric in half widthways. Press the fold lightly, then unfold.

3 Using a chalk pencil or a fading dressmaker's pen, lightly draw a 30 x 40cm rectangle on the right hand side, 6cm in from the fold and right edge, and 6cm up from the bottom edge. Mark three points on the top and bottom lines at 5cm, 15cm and 25cm from the left corners. Mark four points along the side lines at 5cm, 15cm, 25cm and 35cm down from the top corners. Join these dots to form a diamond grid.

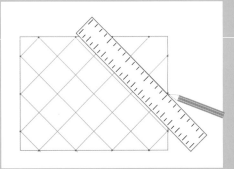

4 Lay 40 of the petals diagonally across the grid, rearranging them until you have a well-balanced layout of pattern and colour. Pin them in place, making sure they all touch at the tips.

top tip CUT OUT EACH OF THE PETALS ALONG THE DIAGONAL, BIAS GRAIN, FOLLOWING THE ARROW ON THE TEMPLATE. THIS PART OF THE FABRIC HAS THE MOST 'GIVE' AND SO THE CURVED EDGES OF THE PETALS WILL LOOK SMOOTH AND CRISP.

Circles
Laundry Bag

5 Slip stitch the petals to the background using small diagonal stitches and a thread that matches the predominant colour of each fabric.

6 To mark the position of the drawstring channel, draw a pencil line 10cm down from the top edge, on the wrong side of the fabric. Bind the top edge and 12cm of each side edge – to just below the pencil line – with the pink bias binding.

7 Cut a 64cm length from the remaining binding and press under a 1cm turning at each end. Pin this along the pencil line, so that the neatened ends are aligned with the side edges. Using white sewing thread, machine stitch along the top and bottom edges of the binding, 2mm from the fold.

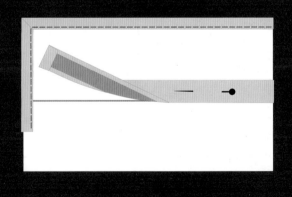

8 Refold the bag widthways and pin the side and bottom edges together. Machine stitch these two edges, leaving a 1cm seam allowance. Start at the bottom corner and end the seam by angling the stitches across the bias binding so that it ends just below the drawstring channel. Neaten the seam allowance with an overlock or zigzag stitch and turn right side out. Press lightly.

9 Fasten a safety pin to one end of the cord, or thread it through a large bodkin. Feed the cord all the way through the drawstring channel, in one opening and out of the other.

10 Tie the ends of the cord together in a loose knot and trim the ends to 10cm. Now it's time to use those two spare petals, to make the tabs. Tack each one over a card template, then leaving the card in place and fold them in half. Starting at the fold, stitch the sides securely together to 5mm from the point. Slip the tab over the end of the cord, securing the point to the cord with a few stitches, then sew the other sides together. Add the other tab in the same way.

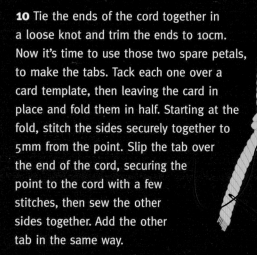

top tip AS A FINISHING TOUCH, MY INITIALS WERE EMBROIDERED IN THE BOTTOM LEFT CORNER WITH FINE CHAIN STITCH, WORKED WITH THREE STRANDS OF THREAD. IF YOU ARE MAKING THIS AS A PRESENT YOU COULD ADD YOUR FRIEND'S MONOGRAM OR NAME.

Floral Washbag

MATERIALS

1m x 10cm green floral print fabric
1m x 10cm pink floral print fabric
30 x 60cm woven waterproof shower
   curtain fabric
25cm white nylon zip
matching sewing thread
sewing kit
sewing machine

CUTTING OUT

from green floral print fabric
twenty 8cm squares
from pink floral print fabric
twenty 8cm squares
two 3 x 4cm zip tabs

SKILL LEVEL: 2

One of the fascinating things about patchwork is the way that you can piece together printed fabrics to create a completely new design. To make this useful zip-up washbag squares were cut from two different colourways of my Lace Stripe cotton duck and then arranged alternately to make a chequerboard pattern, which looks as if it has been woven from lengths of floral braid.

1 Lay out the squares for the (identical) front and back of the bag, in four rows of five. Alternate the colours and the direction of the stripes to create the basketweave effect. With right sides facing, sew the patches together in horizontal rows, leaving a 1cm seam allowance.

2 Press the seam allowances to one side, alternating left and right, as you go down the rows.

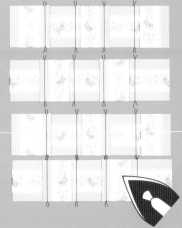

3 Hold the top edge of the second row against the bottom edge of the first row together, with the seam matching and the allowances butting up next to each other. Insert a pin at each seam line and the corners, then machine stitch 1cm from the edge. Add the other two rows, then make up the second panel in the same way.

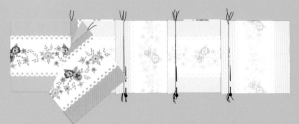

4 Press all the seam allowances open so that the patchwork will lie flat.

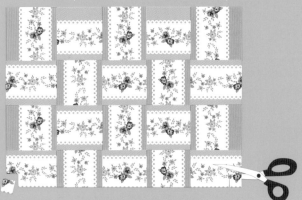

5 Rule a line 2.5cm up from the bottom edge of one panel, then trim along this line. Draw a 2.5cm square at each corner and cut them away. Do the same on the other panel.

top tip THIS VERSATILE DESIGN CAN BE ADAPTED BY ALTERING THE SIZE OF THE SQUARES:

MAKE THEM SMALLER FOR A MAKE-UP BAG OR LARGER FOR A CHANGING BAG (A GREAT BABY SHOWER GIFT!).

Floral Washbag

6 Pin the panels, wrong side down, to the waterproof lining. Machine stitch the two layers together, sewing 3mm from the edge of the panels. Cut out neatly.

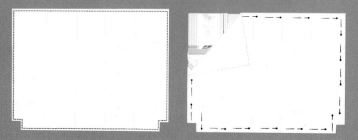

7 With right sides facing, stitch one of the zip tabs across the tapes at the top end of the zip. Press the seam towards the tab. Lay the zip along the top edge of a bag panel to check the size and sew the other tab to the bottom end, so that the outer edge of the tab lines up with the side of the bag. (You can stitch through the teeth without damaging the machine needle, as long as you are using a nylon zip, but avoid the tiny metal stopper at the bottom.)

8 Tack the top edge of one side panel to the zip and tabs with right sides facing. Fit a zip foot to the machine and stitch 6mm from the edge. Sew the other panel to the opposite side, then press the seams lightly and top stitch.

9 Open the zip and fold the bag so that the patchwork lies on the inside. Pin the side and bottom edges together, leaving the squared off corners open. Machine stitch the bottom edge with a 1cm seam, then sew the side edges, starting from the corners and sewing towards the zip. Secure both ends of the three seams with reverse stitches. Lightly press them open.

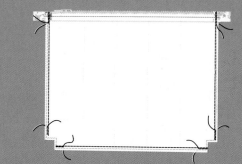

10 Now open out one of the open corners and refold it so that the side seams lines up with the bottom seam. Pin the two edges together and machine stitch with a 6mm seam. Do the same at the other corner, then turn right side out. Ease the corners out to make a flat base for the bag.

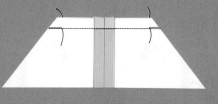

top tip IF YOU ARE A REAL PERFECTIONIST, YOU CAN NEATEN THE INSIDE SEAMS WITH AN OVERLOCKING STITCH OR BY BINDING THEM WITH BIAS BINDING, EITHER BY HAND OR MACHINE.

Dresden Plate Tote Bag

MATERIALS

13cm square each of four different
  floral print fabrics
13cm square each of red, pink and
  blue spot print fabrics
30 x 75cm calico
90m of 2cm-wide cotton tape
scrap paper for template
matching sewing thread
sewing kit
sewing machine

CUTTING OUT

*from floral and red and pink spot
  print fabrics*
six pairs of matching outer petals
from blue spot print fabric
one 12cm circle
from paper
12 inner petals

TEMPLATES

Inner and outer petal shapes
  on page 156
12cm diameter circle

SKILL LEVEL: 1

When planning the giveaway kit for *Patch!*, I was keen to
come up with a design that was both suitable for beginners
and challenging enough for more experienced stitchers. This
'Dresden Plate' tote bag provided the perfect solution. It's
a combination of patchwork, appliqué and hand quilting,
and so makes a good practical introduction to all three
techniques. I've put together an exclusive selection of my
latest floral, paisley and mini spot prints for you to use,
and if you don't need another bag, you can always make
the kit up as a cushion... turn the page to see what I mean!

1 Pin a paper template centrally to the wrong
side of a petal and fold over the surplus fabric
along the two side edges, sewing it down as
you go. Don't worry about the raw ends at
the point, as they will be concealed by the
flower centre. When you come to the curved
edge, make a series of little folds to gather in
the turning. Tack the fabric down with small
stitches and finish off with a double stitch.
Cover all the templates in this way.

2 Lay the twelve petals out in a circle and
decide on their arrangement – you could sew them together
randomly, as shown here, or arrange them so that the
matching petals lie opposite each other.

3 Hold the first two petals together with
right sides facing. Starting at the right
corner, join them with a row
of small over stitches, picking
up just a couple of threads from
the folded fabric on each side. Fasten
off at the end, then join the other petals
to make the whole flower.

4 Press the flower lightly from the wrong side, then unpick
the tacking stitches and remove the templates.

5 Fold the calico in half lengthways. Place the finished flower
centrally on the front, about 2cm up from the fold. Pin it in
place, through the front layer only.

top tip WHEN YOU ARE TACKING THE FABRIC TO THE PAPER TEMPLATE, START OFF WITH THE KNOT
ON THE RIGHT SIDE. THIS WILL MAKE UNPICKING THE THREADS A MUCH QUICKER PROCESS LATER ON.

Dresden Plate
Tote Bag

6 Slip stitch the folded, curved outside edge of the flower to the bag.

7 Now work the quilting that gives the flower its texture and secures it to the bag. Work a line of regularly spaced small stitches about 4mm inside the edge of each petal, starting and ending at the centre.

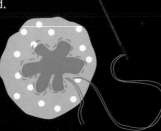

8 Fold back and tack down a 5mm turning around the edge of the blue spot circle, using a double length of thread. Draw it up tightly to make a Suffolk puff and fasten off the end securely.

9 Pin the puff to the centre of the flower to conceal the raw ends, and slip stitch it in place.

10 Fold the bag in half again, with the right side facing inwards. Pin the two sides together and machine stitch, leaving a 1cm allowance. Neaten the raw edges with an overlocking or zigzag stitch.

11 Press back a 5mm turning around the opening, then turn back and pin down a further 2cm to make a double hem. Machine stitch 3mm from the top edge and from the fold.

12 Turn the bag right side out and ease the corners into neat right angles with the point of your embroidery scissors. Press the seams lightly.

13 Cut the tape in half and press under a 5cm turning at each end. Pin the ends of one length to the front of the bag, 6cm in from the corners, so that the folds line up with the lower stitch line. Sew the ends in place with rectangles of machine stitches, reinforced with two diagonal lines worked from corner to corner (see page 21).

14 Make the second handle in the sames way and attach to the bag in the corresponding position at the back.

top tip VARIATIONS ON THIS PATTERN PRODUCED SOME OF THE MOST STUNNING PATCHWORK OF

THE 1920S AND '30S. IF YOU'VE ENJOYED YOUR KIT, WHY NOT THINK ABOUT SEWING A WHOLE QUILT TOP?

Dresden Plate Cushion

MATERIALS
materials and equipment as for the bag
plus
35 x 75cm white cotton fabric
safety standard toy or cushion filling

CUTTING OUT
from calico fabric
one 30 x 35cm front panel
two 30 x 20cm back panels
from white cotton fabric
two 32 x 27 rectangles for cushion pad

SKILL LEVEL: 1

Here's a variation on a theme – an alternative way to make up your kit. The calico is cut into three pieces to make the cover and the tape is turned into two ties to fasten as a bow at the back. The only extras that you'll need are the fabric and filling to make a small cushion pad.

1 Make up the patchwork flower as for steps 1–4 of the Dresden Plate Tote Bag on page 67. Pin it centrally to the front panel and hand sew it in place. Make up the Suffolk puff and stitch it over the raw ends as for steps 6–9.

2 Press under a 5mm turning on one long edge of a back panel, then press under a second 1cm turning to make a double hem. Machine stitch down. Neaten one edge of the other panel in the same way.

3 Lay out the front panel with the right side facing upwards. Place one back panel at side edge, with the right sides downwards and the raw edges matching. Pin together through all the layers and machine stitch all the way round, leaving a 1cm seam allowance.

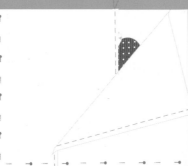

4 Turn the cover right side out and clip a small triangle from each corner, cutting to within 3mm of the stitching. Carefully ease out the corners with your embroidery scissors. Press the seams lightly.

5 Cut the tape into four equal lengths and press under a 5mm turning at one end of each. Pin two of them to the top back panel, 8cm in from the corners, so that the fold lies along the stitched line. Hand stitch in place and snip a small triangle from each loose end.

6 Pin the remaining ties to the other back panel, 5cm away from the first two. Hand sew them in place and trim the ends.

7 Pin the two cushion pad panels together. Machine stitch around the outside edge with a 1cm seam allowance, leaving a 10cm gap in one long edge.

8 Press back the seam allowance along the opening then turn right side out. Clip and ease out the corners as for the cover and press the seams. Stuff firmly with the cushion filling, then close the gap with slip stitch. Put the cushion inside the cover and tie two bows at the back.

top tip IF YOU DON'T WANT TO MAKE YOUR OWN CUSHION, USE A READY-MADE 30CM SQUARE FEATHER OR POLYESTER PAD, WHICH WILL SQUASH UP TO GIVE THE COVER A WELL-FILLED, UPHOLSTERED APPEARANCE.

Rose Linen Pillowcase

MATERIALS
old printed linen cloth
plain linen fabric for back
matching sewing thread
sewing kit
sewing machine

CUTTING OUT
from printed linen fabric
six 28cm squares for front (see step 1)
from linen fabric
one flap: 53 x 20cm
one back panel: 78 x 53cm

I cut these two pieces so that the original hem-stitched edge of the sheet lies along the 53cm sides, which gave me ready-finished edges at the opening. This meant I had to adjust the width of the back panel to 76.5cm and the depth of the flap to 18.5cm.

SKILL LEVEL: 1

As you may know, I have a passion for vintage textiles and have collected them for as long as I can remember. Old fabrics have a special quality that only comes from long use and will last for many more years – even if they show signs of wear, there are usually some areas that can be salvaged. When I came across a rose-bordered tablecloth that was in perfect condition apart from a torn centre, I knew it deserved a new lease of life, so here it is... transformed into a pretty pillowcase and backed with a linen cut from an old sheet.

1 Draw up a 28cm square template on dressmaker's pattern paper to use as your guide for cutting out the patches. Avoiding any damaged areas, cut one square from each corner of the cloth and two squares from the sides. You can mark guidelines on the template to make sure that the printed design will line up across all six squares.

2 Lay the patches out in their finished order. Starting at the bottom row, pin the side edges of the centre square and one of the corner squares together, with right sides facing. Machine stitch, leaving a 1.5cm seam allowance. Sew on the other corner square in the same way, then join the three top patches.

---

top tip THE FINISHED SIZE OF THIS CASE IS 50 X 75CM, SO YOU'LL NEED TO ADJUST THE SIZE OF THE SIX PATCHES TO FIT A LARGER

OR A LONGER RECTANGULAR PILLOW. FOR A SQUARE PILLOW, CUT FOUR SQUARES, ONE FROM EACH CORNER OF THE ORIGINAL CLOTH.

Rose Linen
Pillowcase

3 With right sides facing, place the two pieces together so that the bottom edge of the top row lies against the top row of the bottom row. Line up the seams and pin them at right angles for a precise match. Pin the rest of the seam, and machine stitch 1.5cm from the edge. Press this long seam open.

4 If it isn't already neatened, make a narrow double hem along one long edge of the linen flap. Press under 5mm, then a further 1cm turning and top stitch the fold. Hem one short edge of the back panel as necessary.

5 Pin the long raw edge of the flap to one short edge of the finished front. Machine stitch together, leaving a 1.5cm seam allowance.

6 Lay the front panel out on your work surface with the right side upwards and open out the flap. Position the back panel over it so that the hemmed edge lies along the seam between the flap and the front panel. Turn the flap over the back panel and pin together along the top, bottom and left side edges.

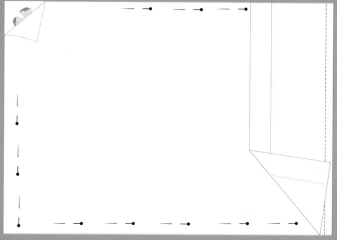

7 Machine stitch the pinned edges, then trim the seam allowance to 6mm. Neaten with a zigzag or overlocking stitch. Turn the pillow case right side out, ease out the corners and press the seams.

top tip IF YOU DON'T HAVE A SUITABLE TABLECLOTH TO UPCYCLE, A LARGE-SCALE PATCHWORK PILLOWCASE WOULD MAKE A GOOD

FOCAL POINT ON YOUR BED: USE 28CM SQUARES CUT FROM SIX DIFFERENT STRIPES, SPOTS OR FLORALS, OR A MIXTURE OF FABRICS.

Boudoir Cushion

MATERIALS

120 x 60cm curtain lining fabric
scraps of floral print fabric
8 buttons
matching sewing thread
sewing kit
25 x 38cm cushion pad

CUTTING OUT

from lining fabric
six 26cm foundation squares
one 27 x 39.5cm back panel
from floral print fabrics
seventeen 7.5cm squares

SKILL LEVEL: 3

This sumptuous cushion is made from 'Cathedral Window' patchwork, the technique where sewing meets origami. It first evolved in the 1930s, when it was also known as 'Daisy Block' or 'Mock Orange Blossom'. The folded, petal-shaped frames provide a showcase for tiny fragments of fabric and some mid-twentieth century charm quilts consist of dozens of cotton prints, all different. My version uses scraps of lingerie silk and rayon from that era, bordered with a soft sateen lining fabric, for a rather more glamorous look.

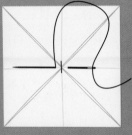

1 Start off by marking a cross on the foundation squares into quarters, as a guideline to help you fold accurately. Fold the side edges together and lightly press the centre crease. Open out, then fold the top and bottom edges together and press the crease. Press a 5mm turning along each edge of the square.

2 With the turnings facing upwards, fold each corner to the centre, so that the edges of the square lie against the guidelines. Press the diagonal folds in turn.

3 Now fold the corner points in once again and press them in place.

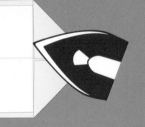

4 Make a tiny cross stitch at the centre of the foundation square, through all the layers, to secure the folds and hold down the points.

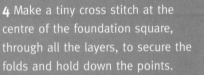

5 Pin the first two foundation squares together with right sides facing and oversew the top edges together, as for paper-covered patchwork (you can check how to do this on page 23). Join on a third square, then sew the remaining three squares together. Pin both along one long edge, with right sides facing, and oversew. Press the completed piece lightly from the wrong side.

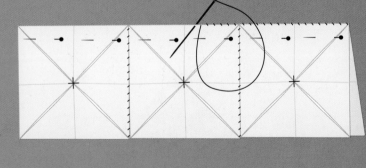

top tip SOME FABRICS I USED IN MY 'WINDOWS' ARE SHEER; I FOUND THE STITCHING BETWEEN THE BLOCKS SHOWED THROUGH.

TO CONCEAL THE JOINS, I POSITIONED 8CM SQUARES OF LEFTOVER LINING FABRIC BEHIND THE FINER SILKS BEFORE FOLDING BACK THE CURVES.

Boudoir Cushion

6 Pin one of the patches to each of the diamond spaces between the squares, making sure that the colours and patterns are balanced.

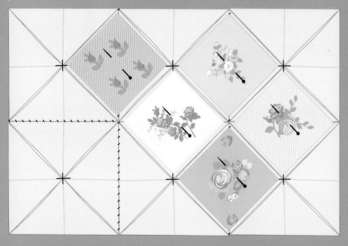

7 Turn back and pin down the foundation squares so that they conceal the edges of the flowered patches and create shallow curves.

8 Slip stitch down the folded edges through all the layers, using matching sewing thread.

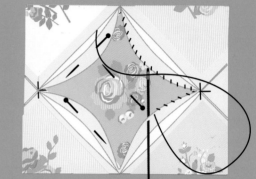

9 To fill in the triangular spaces around the edge, press the remaining patches diagonally in half. Pin them into the gaps and oversew the folds to the outside edges of the foundation squares. Turn back and stitch down the diagonal folds as before to conceal the other two edges.

10 Sew a button to the centre of each of the foundation squares. This not only looks decorative, but will conceal any imperfections in the stitching at the ends of the petals.

11 Make up the cushion by pressing under a 1cm turning all around the back panel. Check that it is the same size as the completed cushion front, adjusting the turnings if necessary, then pin the two together with wrong sides facing. Oversew two long and one short edges, insert the cushion pad, then pin and stitch the opening.

top tip IF YOU ENJOY THIS INTRIGUING TECHNIQUE, WHY NOT GO ON TO MAKE AN ENTIRE QUILT? YOU WON'T HAVE TO BACK OR LINE THE COMPLETED BLOCKS SO IT WILL BE QUICK TO DO, AND BECAUSE IT'S ALL HAND-STITCHED, YOUR WORK WILL BE VERY PORTABLE.

Crazy Patch Cushion

MATERIALS

selection of embroidered cloths
50cm square white linen fabric for
    cushion front
40cm square gingham fabric for
    cushion back
170cm pink bias binding
170cm fine piping cord
40cm square cushion pad
matching sewing thread
2 skeins pink stranded cotton
    embroidery thread
sewing kit

SKILL LEVEL: 3

Women of past generations spent hours patiently stitching household textiles – tray cloths, dressing table mats, napkins and runners – which we seldom use today. Rather than storing these away in a drawer, I wanted to show them off and give the fine embroidery a new lease of life. This crazy patchwork cushion, which uses sections salvaged from a collection of old linens, is my tribute to the work of our grandmothers.

1 Sort through your fabrics, picking out the most interesting areas of embroidery. Cut each patch into a multi-sided shape, with straight edges.

2 Draw a 40cm square in the centre of the white linen cushion front, ruling each line from side to side or top to bottom. Starting in the middle, arrange the patches on the white linen, in a crazy paving style. Overlap the edges to cover the square completely, then pin them in place.

3 Tuck under a 5mm turning along each of the uppermost edges and sew the patches to the linen, with small slip stitches worked in white sewing thread, as close to the folds as possible.

4 Redraw the 40cm square, going over the edges of the patches where they overlap the outline.

top tip WASH AND PRESS ALL THE CLOTHS AND DISCARD ANY WORN OR STAINED AREAS. YOU MAY FIND THAT THE COLOUR OF THE FABRIC MAY VARY FROM SNOW WHITE TO CREAM BUT THIS ONLY ADDS TO ITS CHARM.

Crazy Patch Cushion

5 Thread a long-eyed needle with three strands of pink embroidery thread and stitch a row of feather stitch (see how to do this on page 29) over each folded edge. Make sure that the outer rows of stitching end 5mm from the pencilled outline.

6 Cut the cushion front to size by trimming along the pencil lines. Press back a 1cm turning along each edge. Mitre the corners (see page 21) and then tack down the turning.

7 Prepare the piping by folding the bias binding over the cord and tacking the two sides together. Fit a zip foot to your sewing machine and sew a line of straight stitch close to the cord (this will keep the piping stable when you hand stitch the cover).

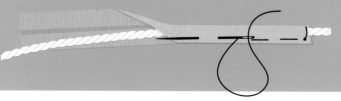

8 Starting close to one corner, pin the piping around the edge of the cover so that the cord peeps over the edge. Hand sew in place with white sewing cotton. Leave the first 3cm unstitched, and make small, closely spaces slip stitches all round the four edges. When you have completed the round, fold the two ends to the back so that they butt up closely against each other. Sew down on the wrong side and trim to 2cm.

9 Press back 1cm around cushion back, mitring the corners as for the front.

10 Pin the back and front together and slip stitch the cushion back in place around three sides, sewing through the bias binding. Insert the cushion pad, then sew up the final side.

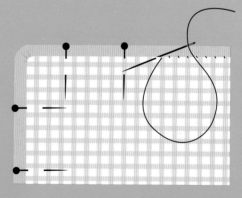

top tip SAVE YOUR TINIEST OFFCUTS OF PRINTED AND PLAIN FABRIC FROM YOUR OTHER PROJECTS

AND USE THEM TO CREATE A MORE BRIGHTLY PATTERNED INTERPRETATION OF THIS THRIFTY TECHNIQUE.

Triangle Patch Pillowcase

MATERIALS

a selection of striped and gingham
   cotton fabrics in reds, blues
   and white
a cotton shirt with button front
red and white gingham for backing
matching sewing thread
quilter's ruler
rotary cutter and cutting mat
soft pencil and ruler
sewing kit
sewing machine

SKILL LEVEL: 2

The country-style colour scheme of red, blue and white
has been reinterpreted many times over the years. To give
this pillowslip a crisper, more contemporary look, I chose a
repeating triangle design that was made up in cotton salvaged
from check and striped clothing. To save a lot of fiddly
stitching, I recycled a shirt front to make the buttoned opening.

1 Wash and press all the fabrics, then cut out eighteen dark
and eighteen light 14cm squares. Using a ruler and a sharp,
soft pencil, draw a diagonal line across each of the light
squares, from corner to corner. With right sides facing, pin
them together in pairs, one light and one dark. Machine stitch
two parallel lines across the square, each one 6mm from the
line. Cut the squares apart along the line.

2 Trim the patches down to 11.5cm square, then press all
the seam allowances towards the darker patches. Lay them
out in five horizontal rows of seven squares, with all the
dark triangles pointing towards the bottom right corner.
Take time to rearrange them until the colours and patterns
are evenly balanced.

3 Join the squares in vertical rows of five, starting at the top
left corner. Pin the first two patches together with right sides
facing, so that the bottom edge of the first square lies along
the top edge of the second one. Machine stitch, leaving a
seam allowance of 6mm, then join on the other three patches
in the same way. Double check that all the dark triangles are
facing in the same direction, as it's very easy to get them the
wrong way round at this stage!

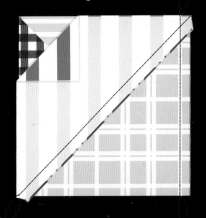

top tip THE PILLOWSLIP IS QUICKLY ASSEMBLED USING A ROTARY CUTTER AND QUILTER'S RULER

TO MAKE THE 'HALF SQUARE TRIANGLE' PATCHES. LEARN HOW TO USE A ROTARY CUTTER ON PAGE 17.

Triangle Patch Pillowcase

4 When the row is complete, press all the straight seam allowances towards the first square. Join the other six rows in the same way.

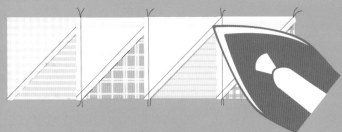

5 Now join the rows together. With right sides facing, hold the left edge of the first row against the right edge of the second row, matching the seams exactly. Insert a pin at each seam line and at both corners.

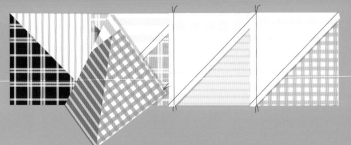

6 Machine stitch 6mm from the edge, then add the other five rows. Press all the seams in the same direction, towards the right.

7 Cut a rectangle of gingham to exactly the same size as the completed patchwork. This will be the back of the pillowslip.

8 Trim the buttonhole and button bands from one of the shirts. Each strip should be 6cm wide and as long as possible.

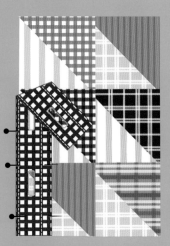

9 With right sides facing, pin the buttonhole strip to the left edge of the patchwork front and machine stitch with a 6mm seam allowance. Neaten the seam with a zig zag or overlocking stitch and press away from the buttonholes.

10 Pin the button band to the back, this time with the wrong side of the band lying along the right side of the pillowslip. Check that the buttons will line up exactly with the buttonholes, then sew in place and neaten the seam.

11 With right sides facing pin the top, right and bottom edges of the front and back together. Machine stitch 6mm from the edge and neaten the seam. Turn right side out, ease out the corners and press the side seams.

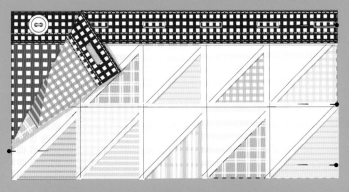

top tip TO MAKE THE BUTTON BAND LOOK A BIT MORE INTERESTING, I SNIPPED OFF THE ORIGINAL BUTTONS AND SEWED ON A MULTI-COLOURED SELECTION SAVED FROM THE OTHER SHIRTS I HAD COLLECTED.

Suffolk Puff Cushion

MATERIALS

120 x 40cm red spot print fabric
120 x 25cm blue spot print fabric
about 100 x 25cm in floral prints with
   a white background
94 x 42cm plain blue cotton fabric
tea bags
washing-up bowl
wooden spoon
matching sewing thread
sewing machine
sewing kit
40cm square cushion pad

CUTTING OUT
from red spot print fabric
45 circles
from blue spot print fabric
16 circles
from other print fabrics
20 circles

SKILL LEVEL: 3

When I discovered a square of Suffolk Puff patchwork amidst a bundle of vintage textiles I decided the pretty, softly faded fabrics needed a second chance. The panel was stitched to the front of a plain pink cushion and I was delighted with the way the unexpectedly bright colour peeped out through the spaces between the puffs. This inspired me to create a cushion cover from my own spot, star and floral haberdashery fabrics, but to keep the softness of the original piece I first dipped all the fabric in strong tea to tone down the colours.

1 Launder any new fabrics to remove the dressing used in the manufacturing process. Make up a dye bath by steeping five tea bags (traditional strong English breakfast tea rather anything fruity or herbal!) in a washing up bowl of very hot water. Remove them after about fifteen minutes.

2 Add the fabrics and leave them to soak for thirty minutes, stirring them with a wooden spoon now and again to ensure even coverage. Rinse, then leave to dry naturally and press well. Remember that the fabric will dry to a lighter shade, so if you would like it to be darker, just go through the whole process again.

3 Trace an 11cm diameter template on to paper and use this as a guide to cut out the fabric circles, as listed above.

4 Thread a long needle with a long length of thread and knot the ends together so that it is double.

5 To make a circle of fabric into a puff, fold back a 5mm turning around the circumference and stitch it down with a round of evenly spaced running stitches. The smaller the stitches, the finer your gathers will be: the ones used for the cushion shown here were 8mm long with equal gaps between them.

6 Gently draw up the thread to gather the circle, using the tip of your needle to push the raw edges inside if necessary. Take the needle down through the finished puff and fasten off the thread securely on the wrong side with a few short back stitches. Trim the thread close to the surface.

top tip SUFFOLK PUFFS CAN BE STITCHED TOGETHER IN MANY DIFFERENT WAYS: TRY ARRANGING THEM IN

STRAIGHT ROWS, A CHEQUERBOARD PATTERN, DIAGONAL LINES OR JUST HAPHAZARDLY FOR A LESS FORMAL LOOK.

Suffolk Puff Cushion

7 Arrange the finished puffs in nine rows of nine, with the red spot ones around the outside edge and forming a central cross. Each corner then has five white and four blue spot puffs.

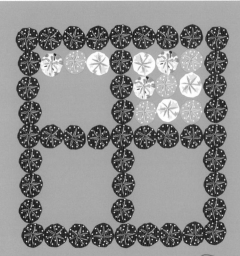

8 Sew together the top row of puffs. Hold the first two together with right sides facing and make several small, tight overstitches to join the edges together. Take the needle to the opposite side of the puff and sew on the next one in the same way. Do the same all the way along the row, making sure that the stitches all lie in a straight line, then fasten off securely. Join the other eight rows in the same way and lay them back out the the right order.

9 Now comes the tricky bit: joining the rows. Start by holding the top two rows together with right sides facing. Join the first puff of each row with a few stitches, then take the needle across to the bottom edge of the second row. Sew this point to the first puff of the third row, then repeat the process so that all the first puffs are stitched together.

10 Join all the second puffs, then the third, and continue until the cover is completed. Check it for any weak joins and re-stitch tightly.

11 Turn under and press a 1cm double hem at each short end of the blue fabric rectangle.

12 Place the fabric face upwards on your work surface and turn back 25cm at each edge. Pin the top and bottom edges together through all the layers and machine stitch, leaving a 1cm seam allowance.

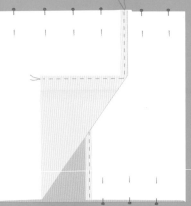

13 Turn the cover right side out and press. Place it face down on the finished puff cushion front, adjusting the position so that half a circle projects at each edge. Pin the cover to the cushion front and slip stitch the two together around the edge of the cover. Insert the cushion pad.

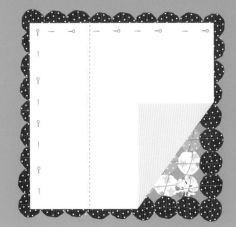

---

top tip IF YOU'RE NOT A TEA DRINKER, DON'T WORRY. STRONG, FRESHLY BREWED COFFEE CAN

ALSO BE USED TO CHANGE THE COLOUR OF YOUR FABRIC, AND WILL GIVE IT A WARMER, BROWNER TONE.

Child's Cushion

MATERIALS

a minimum of
   60 x 40cm check fabric
   40 x 10cm small-scale floral fabric
   40 x 10cm large-scale floral fabric
old envelopes and paper
matching sewing thread
sewing machine
sewing kit
25cm cushion pad

TEMPLATES

from check fabric
one 10cm square
two 16 x 26cm back panels
from small-scale floral print fabric
four 10cm squares
from large-scale floral print fabric
four 10cm squares
from paper
nine 8cm square templates

SKILL LEVEL: 1

This simple cushion cover, made from nine bright squares, pays homage to one of the first sewing projects I did as a little girl. I can vividly remember sitting patiently as I completed each fabric-covered template in turn, and then the huge sense of achievement when I learnt how to stitch them together. It would still be a perfect starting point for beginners or for newcomers to English-style patchwork.

1 Thread your needle and keep it ready to hand. Pin a paper square centrally to the back of one of the fabric squares so that there is a 1cm margin all round.

2 Fold the top margin back over the template. Starting with the knot on the right side, sew the fabric to the paper with long running stitches. Fold over the next margin so that you have a neat right angle at the corner. Tack down this edge, then stitch down the other two edges. Work a double stitch to secure the thread and trim the end to 2cm. Cover all the papers in the same way.

4 Pick up the first two squares on the top row. With the fabric sides facing, hold them together so that the left edge of the second square lies along the right edge of the first square. (Don't worry, this will make sense when you do it!)

5 Starting at the right hand corner, sew the two patches together with small over stitches.

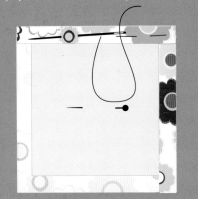

3 Using the photograph opposite as your guide, lay the squares out in three rows of three, with the check patch in the centre surrounded by the eight flowery patches.

6 Join the third square to complete the row, then make up the other two rows.

top tip MAKING UP THE CUSHION COVER BY MACHINE IS A REALLY JOB FOR TEENAGERS AND ADULTS, BUT IT WOULD BE A GOOD SEWING LESSON FOR OLDER CHILDREN WORKING UNDER CLOSE SUPERVISION, AS THE SEAMING IS VERY STRAIGHTFORWARD.

Child's Cushion

7 Now it's time to sew the three rows together in just the same way, making sure that the seam lines match up as you go. When you get to the end of the thread, make three stitches in the opposite direction to secure the end of the seam and trim the tail to 5mm.

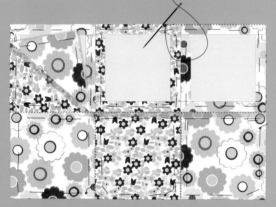

8 Then you have finished sewing, unpick and remove all the papers, then open out the turnings around the outside edge. Press these so that they lie flat.

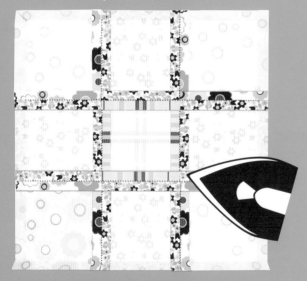

9 Press under a 1cm double turning along one long edge of each back panel. Sew this down by hand or machine.

10 Place the cushion front on your work surface with the right side facing upwards. Position one back panel, face downwards, on the left of the cushion front so that the raw edges are matching. Lay the other panel on the right, then pin the layers together around all four sides.

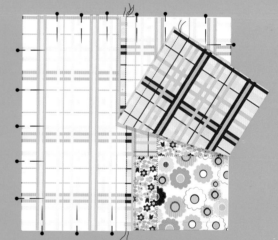

11 Machine stitch all the way around the edge of the cushion cover, leaving a 1cm seam allowance.

12 Snip a tiny triangle from each corner, 5mm from the stitching. Turn it right side out and ease out the corners into sharp angles with a pencil. Press the seams lightly then insert the cushion pad.

top tip MAKE THIS CUSHION INTO A SOUVENIR OF CHILDHOOD BY USING SCRAPS OF FABRIC FROM OUTGROWN SHIRTS, BLOUSES AND DRESSES. THEN SEW ON A FEW BUTTONS, BUTTONS OR EMBROIDERED MOTIFS FROM THE GARMENTS AS EXTRA DECORATION.

Child's Pentagon Ball

MATERIALS
twelve scraps of cotton, at least
   15cm square
used envelopes or old letters
tacking thread
matching sewing thread
250g polyester toy stuffing
sewing kit

SKILL LEVEL: 2

Every budding sports star has to start somewhere, so this soft patchwork ball is guaranteed to provide hours of goal practice for your favourite toddler. It's made from twelve hand-stitched pentagons – a variation on the usual honeycomb hexagon technique – and the pictorial fabrics are a blend of vintage nursery finds and my own prints for children.

1 Trace or photocopy the full-size pentagon template on page 156. Using this as your guide, cut out twelve pentagons from recycled paper.

2 Pin a paper pentagon to the wrong side of the first fabric scrap, centring it over either a motif or an interesting pattern area. Cut the fabric to the same pentagon shape but adding a margin, snipping approximately 1cm from the edges of the paper. Fold the fabric margin over each side of the paper pentagon in turn, stitching it to the paper as you go.

3 The ball is made in two separate halves. When you have covered all the papers, plan the layout for both parts. Choose the two strongest motifs and arrange five patches around each one, balancing the colours evenly on each side.

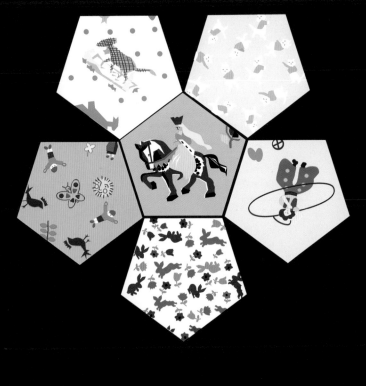

top tip THE FINISHED BALL MEASURES ABOUT 15CM IN DIAMETER, BUT YOU CAN CHANGE THE SIZE OF THE TEMPLATE TO MAKE IT LARGER OR SMALLER: 2.5CM PENTAGONS WOULD MAKE A TINY BALL THAT YOU COULD USE FOR A CHRISTMAS DECORATION.

96

Child's Pentagon Ball

4 Pick out the centre pentagon and one from the edge, and hold them together with right sides facing. Bring a threaded needle out through the right corner of the front patch, then oversew them along one edge. Work a few extra stitches at each end of the row to reinforce the seam.

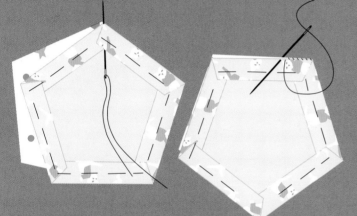

5 Sew the third patch to the next edge of the centre pentagon in the same way. To join the second and third patches, fold the centre patch in half so that the other two face each other and stitch the two adjacent edges together. Join on the remaining three patches in the same way, then make up the second half of the ball.

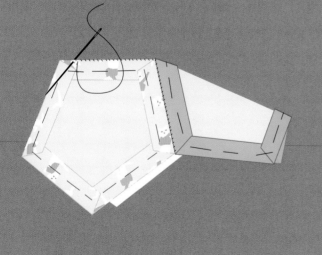

6 Seam the two halves together, remembering to reinforce all corners. At this stage the ball can be a bit awkward to hold, so fold it whichever way feels comfortable for you and adjust the two parts as you sew each pair of sides together. Leave the last two edges unstitched.

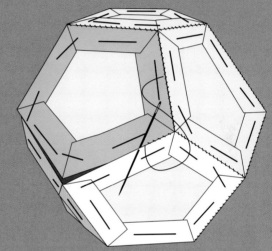

7 Unpick all the paper pentagons and remove. Turn the ball right side out through the gap and stuff with wadding. Carry on filling it until the ball has a good round shape, then over stitch the gap to close.

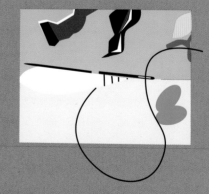

top tip CHOOSE A POLYESTER TOY FILLING THAT MEETS SAFETY STANDARDS AND USE THE HANDLE OF A WOODEN SPOON TO PACK IT DOWN. REMEMBER THAT TO MAKE A GOOD, SOLID BALL IT MAY TAKE MORE STUFFING THAN YOU EXPECT.

Stanley Toy

MATERIALS
dress-weight cotton in mixed prints
scrap of black felt or leather
7 litres of polyester toy filling
two 2cm black buttons
sewing machine
sewing kit

TEMPLATES
Trace off or photocopy the full size triangle, nose and ear templates on page 157.

CUTTING OUT
from mixed print fabrics
one hundred 7cm squares
ten triangles
five 7 x 10cm rectangles
from red spot fabric
four ears
from felt or leather
one nose

SKILL LEVEL: 3

As you may have already guessed, this one of my favourite projects of all... a patchwork version of my dog Stanley. I have to admit that he's almost as adorable as the original, but much better behaved! He's made from an eclectic mix of my lightweight haberdashery fabrics in reds and blues, including dots, flowers, cowboys and, of course, my pet's very own signature print – Mini Stanley.

The seam allowance throughout is 6mm.

1 Cuddly Stanley is made from two dog-shaped side panels (one the mirror image of the other) which are joined together with a gusset loop. Start by laying out 35 squares and five triangles as shown to make the left-facing side panel. With right sides, facing pin and stitch together the patches in each horizontal row.

2 Iron the seam allowances on the top row towards the left, then press the seams on the next row down towards the right. Press all the other rows, alternating the direction in which they lie. The muzzle seams go to the right, as do the top two leg rows. The bottom leg rows lie on the left.

3 To assemble the body, pin the bottom edge of the top head row to the top edge of the next row down, matching up the seams. Machine stitch. Press this and all the other horizontal seams downwards.

4 Now join the head to the top row of the body. Add the muzzle, the other two body rows, the two legs and the tail. Make up the right-facing body panel in exactly the same way, reversing the direction.

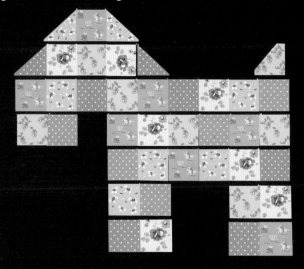

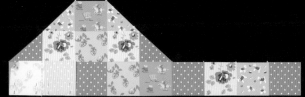

5 With right sides facing, pin the ears together in pairs and sew around the curved edges. Trim the seam back to 3mm at the tips. Turn right side out, and press. Tack in place at the top of the head.

top tip SAFETY FIRST: I'M SURE I DON'T HAVE TO REMIND YOU THAT ANY FILLING USED FOR SOFT TOYS SHOULD CONFORM TO RECOGNISED SAFETY STANDARDS, AND THAT THIS TOY IS FOR OLDER CHILDREN ONLY.

6 The gusset is a mixture of squares and rectangles. The rectangles lie next to the triangular patches at head and tail, and the squares next to the other body squares. Each of the 16 straight edges are assembled separately, then they are joined to make a loop.

7 Start at the tail and join six squares for Stan's back end. Seam two squares for the back paw, two squares for the inside leg, two squares for Stan's underbelly, and so on until you reach the tip of his nose. Seam two rectangles for his forehead, pick a single patch for the crown, two rectangles for the back of his head, three squares for his back and the final rectangle for his tail. Press the seams in one direction. Lay all the pieces in place around the left-facing body panel.

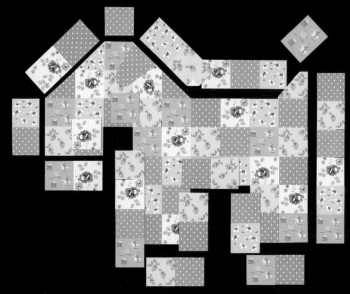

8 Insert a marker pin in the top patch of the first strip so you can find it again. With right sides facing, pin the top of the sole strip to the bottom end. Sew together, leaving 6mm unstitched at each end of the seam. Join the rest of the strips and single patches in the same way, then join to make a loop. Press the seams open.

9 Again starting at the tip of the tail, pin the loop to the body with right sides facing. Fold out the open ends of the seams so that the gusset will fit neatly at the corners. Sew all the way round, 6mm from the edge. Attach the right-facing body panel in the same way, leaving the underbelly unstitched.

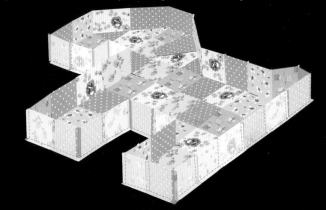

10 Turn right side out and push out the corners. Pack the toy filling down into the paws, muzzle and tail, then into the head and body, using the handle of a wooden spoon to push it down firmly. Slip stitch the opening with a double length of thread.

11 Sew the two eyes very securely to sides of the head and stitch the nose in place with small over stitches.

12 Make a collar from a 35 x 10cm strip of red cotton fabric. Press in half widthways, then press under a 1cm turning at both long edges. Refold and top stitch 3mm from each edge. Fold under the edges and fit around Stan's neck. Trim the ends to fit snugly, then sew them together.

top tip AS A FINISHING TOUCH I HAD A BONE-SHAPED DOG TAG ENGRAVED WITH STAN'S NAME AND ATTACHED IT TO THE FABRIC COLLAR. YOUR LOCAL KEY-CUTTER SHOULD HAVE SOMETHING SIMILAR.

Bunny Blanket

MATERIALS

45cm square 10-count canvas
tapestry frame
fringed cream blanket
15 x 13cm blue felt
matching sewing thread
scrap of orange felt
small amount of polyester toy filling
stranded embroidery thread in green
  and black
tracing paper and pencil
sewing kit

TEMPLATES

Bunny, see page 158

SKILL LEVEL: 1

I like this adorable rabbit patch so much that I have used it twice, adapting it in two quite different ways. Here is its first appearance, cut from blue felted wool, gently padded and appliquéd to the corner of a vintage cream blanket. Have a look at the other version on page 141 – a flowery bunny (or two) would look equally good on the blanket and you could alter the size to make a whole rabbit family.

1 Trace or photocopy the full-sized bunny template on page 158 and cut out around the outside edge. Pin to the felt, then cut out as close to the paper as possible.

2 Pin the bunny to the corner of the blanket. Sew it down by hand with tiny over stitches, leaving 3cm open in the centre of the back.

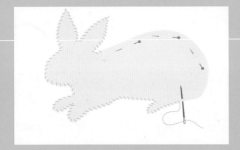

3 Stuff small amounts of polyester filling through this space, using a pencil to push them right into the head, paws and tail end, then sew up the gap.

4 Embroider the eyes and nose in satin stitch (see page 28), using a single thread of black embroidery cotton. Add a few short black straight stitches for the bunny's whiskers.

5 Using blue thread, work curved rows of small running stitches at the front and back legs as indicated on the template. Cut out a little carrot from orange felt and sew it down around the edge with matching thread. Add a tuft of long, thin green chain stitches or several straight stitches to the top of the carrot (see page 29).

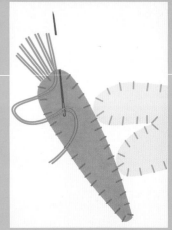

6 To make the tail, carefully snip off one strand of the fringe from the outside edge of the blanket (preferably on the opposite side to the bunny). Curl it up into an oval and stab stitch securely in place.

top tip THE RAISED TAIL AND WOOLLEN FRINGE MEAN THAT THIS TYPE OF DECORATED BLANKET SHOULD BE GIVEN ONLY TO OLDER CHILDREN (AS THERE MAY BE A CHOKING HAZARD FOR SMALL BABIES).

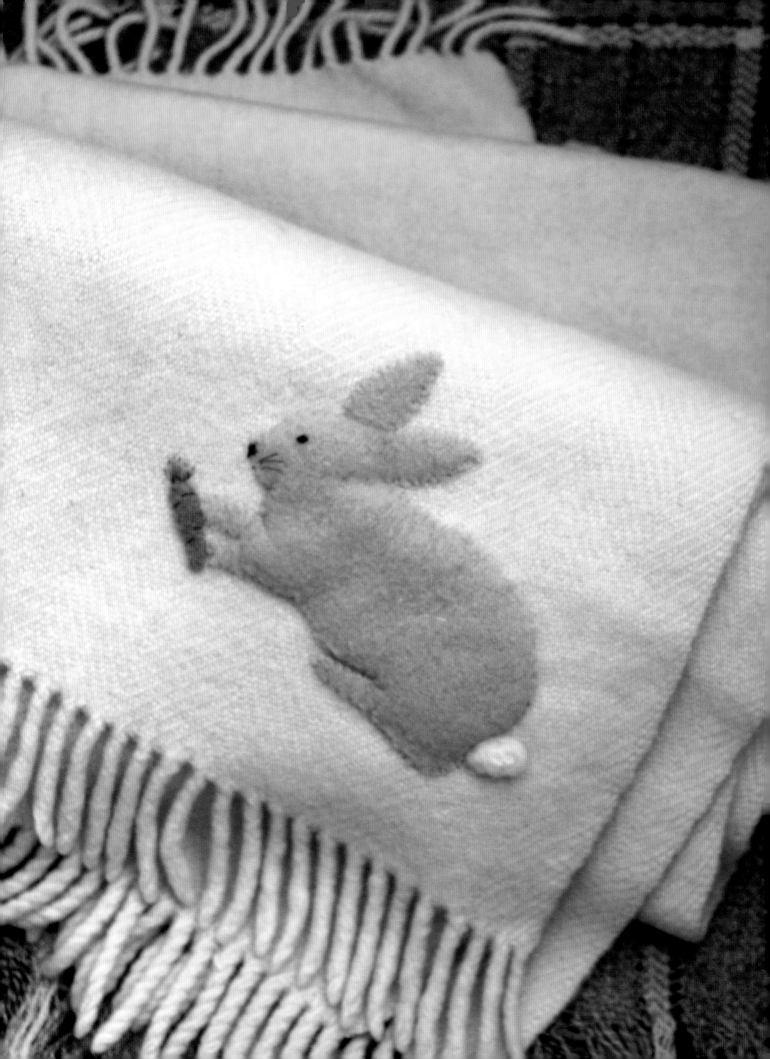

Star Throw

MATERIALS

for each block

45cm square of white cotton fabric

25 x 20cm each of four different print fabrics

10cm square darker fabric

10cm square fusible bonding web

printed fabric for binding

matching sewing thread

sewing kit

sewing machine

CUTTING OUT

for each star

eight star points, two from each fabric

for the binding

one 8cm wide strip, 10cm longer than the sum of all four sides (join separate strips to the required length with a 6mm seam, the press the seams open.)

TEMPLATES

Trace or photocopy the star point template on page 159 and transfer the outline on to thin cardboard.

MEASURING UP

twenty blocks set in 4 rows of 5 = 180 x 220: adapt these proportions to suit your own bed

---

SKILL LEVEL: 3

An ideal bedcover for sunny summer days, this throw is a contemporary re-working of a classic design. It consists of just a single layer of fabric, bound at the edge and decorated with a repeating pattern of patchwork stars. These are a variation on the 'Dresden Plate' pattern and because each star is stitched to an individual square block the finished size can be as as large or small as you wish.

1 Referring to the template, mark the two dots that indicate the seam line on each top corner of the star point patches.

2 Arrange eight patches in their finished star shape. With right sides facing, pin the first two together along one long edge. Machine stitch as far as the dot, then work a few backwards stitches to secure the seam and trim the thread. Add the other six patches in this way, then join the first and last together to complete the star.

3 Press all the seams open and press back a 6mm turning along each outer edge.

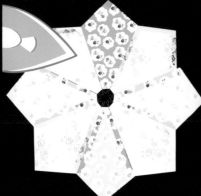

4 Neaten the edge of the white square with an overlocking or zigzag stitch. Press it very lightly in half, then half again to mark it into quarters. Pin the finished star to the square, lining the points up with the crease lines. Sew in place, either by hand or with a narrow machine buttonhole or zigzag stitch.

---

top tip THE STARS ON MY THROW ARE ALL IDENTICAL, BUT THIS DESIGN LOOKS EQUALLY

EFFECTIVE WHEN EACH SQUARE HAS A DIFFERENT STAR MADE FROM EIGHT RANDOMLY SELECTED PRINTS.

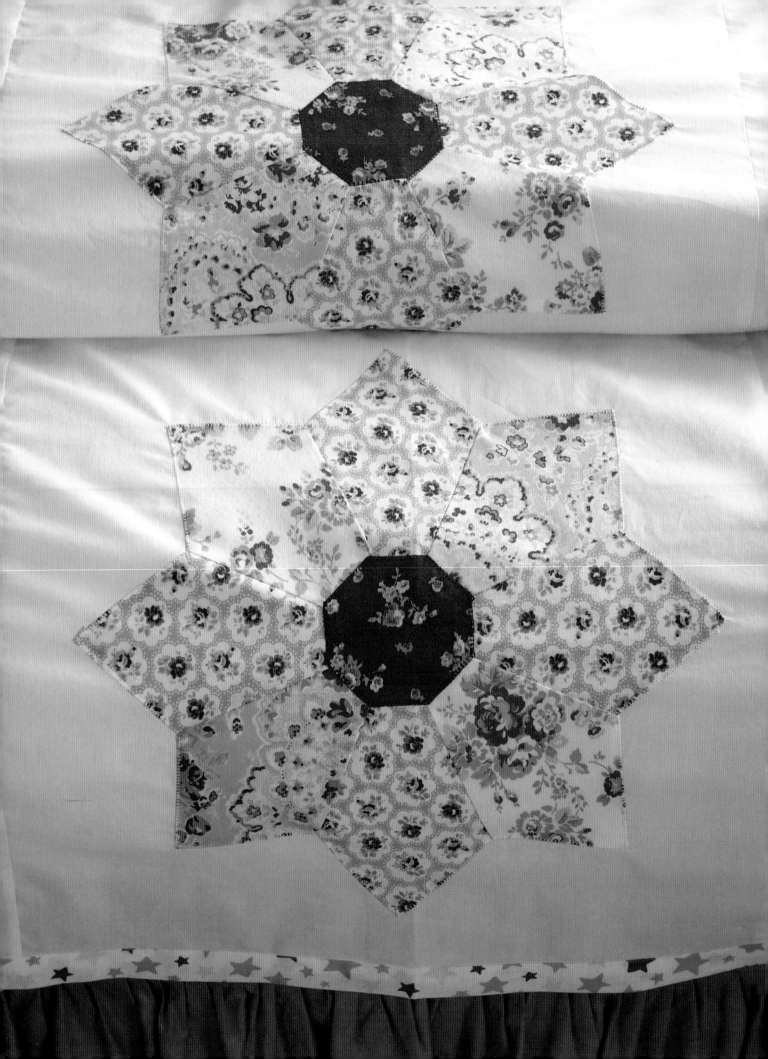

Star
Throw

5 Trace the octagon outline from the template on page 159 on to the paper side of the bonding web. Iron it to the back of the dark fabric and cut out carefully around the outline. Peel off the backing paper and position the patch in the centre of the star. Press in place then machine stitch around the edge in a thread to match the fabric. Make up all the squares in this way.

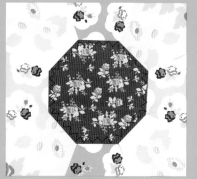

6 Lay out all your finished squares. With right sides facing, join them in horizontal rows with a 1cm seam. Press all the seams open.

7 Again with right sides facing, pin the bottom edge of the top row to the top edge of the second row, matching the seams exactly. Machine stitch and press the seam open. Add the other rows in the same way.

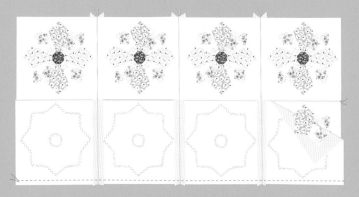

8 Press under a 1cm turning one long edge of the binding strip. With right sides facing, and raw edges matching pin it along the top edge of the throw, trimming the ends in line with the fabric. Machine stitch, then turn the folded edge over to the back. Pin it down so that the fold lies 3mm beyond the stitch line. Machine stitch in place from the front, sewing along the seam line between the throw and the binding. Bind the bottom edge in the same way.

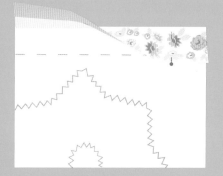

9 When binding the side edges, fold under 1cm at each end of the fabric strip, and pin it down so that the folds project 1mm beyond the edges. Machine stitch and fold over as before, then stitch down from the front. Slip stitch the edges of the folds.

top tip USE AN OLD WHITE SHEET – COTTON OR LINEN – FOR THE BACKING SQUARES

AS AN ECO-ALTERNATIVE TO BUYING NEW FABRIC.

Hankie Bedcover

MATERIALS
printed hankies
flat sheet to fit finished cover
matching sewing thread
sewing machine
sewing kit

SKILL LEVEL: 2

The Stone Roses hankie is far to pretty to be hidden away in a handbag or tucked away in a pocket. The design is an adaptation of one of my fabrics, with a deep curved border of blooms set around a central spray, and it is just one of a series of printed handkerchiefs. I love the way that new shapes are created when the pattern is repeated (see the picture on the previous pages), but the same technique would work equally well with an assortment of different designs.

HOW MANY HANKIES?
The hankies are 50cm square. You will need 3 rows of 5 for a single bed, 4 rows of 5 for a double, 5 rows of 5 for a king size and as many as 6 rows of 5 for a super king. Measure up your bed first and decide how much of an overhang you would like at each side, then round off to the nearest 50cm.

1 Prepare the hankies by removing the labels, then laundering and pressing them. Wash and iron the backing sheet too if it's a new one, then there's no possibility of shrinkage in the future.

2 Join them first in short rows of three or more. Pin together with right sides facing and machine stitch 1cm from the hem. Press the seams open.

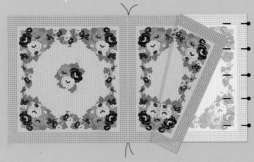

3 Lay the first two rows together along one long edge, again with right sides facing, and line up the seams. Insert a pin through each point where they meet, then pin the rest of the

edges together. Stitch and press as before, and continue until you have joined all the rows.

4 You'll need plenty of space for this step, so make sure you have a nice clean floor! Spread out and smooth the sheet. Place the hankies face down on top, lining the two up along one side and the bottom edge. Pin them together with the pins parallel to the hems, and trim the sheet to the same size as the hankies.

5 Machine stitch all the way round, leaving a 1cm seam allowance. Leave a 50cm gap along one edge and turn the cover right side out through this opening. Press back a 1cm turning along each side of the opening, pin the two layers together and slip stitch to close.

top tip I KNOW THAT IT'S NOT REALLY A PATCH PROJECT, BUT A SINGLE HANDKERCHIEF MAKES A GREAT CUSHION COVER! IMAGINE A WHOLE ROW OF THEM, EACH ONE IN A DIFFERENT FLORAL OR GREETINGS PRINT.

Curtain Panel

MATERIALS

floral fabric

striped fabric for the sashing, plus
   extra for the header and facing

plain fabric

10cm curtain header tape the same
   width as finished curtain

curtain hooks

matching sewing thread

sewing machine

sewing kit

SKILL LEVEL: 3

Like some of the best patchwork, this curtain is a combination
of old and new fabrics. Large patches cut from the bouquets
on my extravagant Blooms furnishing print are sashed with
strips of vintage flannel shirting and offset with small squares
of plain red cotton. The panel is unlined, so the various
materials take on a wonderful stained glass-like quality
when hung against a sunlit window.

HOW MUCH FABRIC?

First measure up to find the finished size of your curtain.
The drop or length will be the distance between the bottom
of your curtain pole and the window sill or floor. The width
will be one and a half times the length of the pole for a single
panel, or one and a half times half the width for each curtain
of a pair.

For the curtain you'll need 12cm of 136cm wide plain, 35cm
of 136cm wide striped and at least 50cm of 148cm wide floral
fabric for each finished square metre (more if you want to
include a lot of very flowery patches).

For the facings you'll need enough striped fabric to make two
8cm strips the same depth as the curtain, one 8cm strip the
same width and one 12 cm strip the same width. You can join
the fabric as necessary to create the right length.

CUTTING OUT

Cut the plain fabric into 8cm squares and the striped into
eight 20cm rectangles with the stripe running lengthways.
Cut the floral print into 20 cm squares, selecting different
areas of the repeat for each one. Approximately 1 square
metre of patchwork requires 16 large squares, 28 rectangular
sashing strips and 16 small squares.

1 Lay all the large squares out and shuffle them around so
that the more densely patterned ones are at the centre and
there is a border of leaves and sprigs. Add in the squares and
rectangles that make up the sashing. You will need sashing
rows at the side and bottom edges to frame the panel, but
not at the top edge.

2 Start by sewing together the
horizontal rows of squares and
rectangles in pairs. Pin the short
ends of each patch together with
right sides facing, then machine stitch
leaving a 1cm seam allowance. You
can speed up the process by chain
piecing and then snipping them apart.

3 Join these pairs together, again
with right sides facing and with a
1cm seam. Sew the final square of each row to the end of the
last rectangle.

top tip IF YOU ARE MAKING A CURTAIN AS LARGE AS MINE, TRY TO PIECE IT ALL IN A SINGLE

SESSION, OR LEAVE THE PATCHES LAID OUT IN A PLACE WHERE THE LAYOUT WON'T BE DISTURBED.

4 Press all the seam allowances so that they lie towards the rectangles.

5 Now join the vertical rectangles to the large squares, in horizontal rows, again with a 1cm seam. Start at the left of each row and join on one patch at a time. Sew the last rectangle in each row to the right edge of the final square.

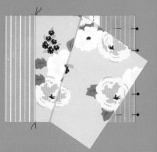

6 When each row is complete, press the seam allowances towards the rectangles.

7 Starting at the bottom, sew the patches and sashing together. Place the first two rows together with right sides facing, so that the top edge of the sashing lies along the bottom edge of the patches. Insert a pin through both seams at the points where they meet. Pin the corners and the spaces between the pins, then machine stitch with a 1cm seam allowance. Press the seam towards the sashing. Join all the rows in this way.

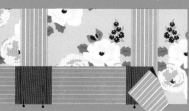

Curtain Panel

8 Cut an 8cm strip of striped fabric to fit along the bottom edge to make the facing. Press under a 6mm turning along one long edge. Pin the raw edge to the curtain with right sides facing and machine stitch with a 1cm seam. Turn the facing to the wrong side, pin and tack down the turning and machine stitch from the right side, close to the long seam line. Press.

10 Cut a 12cm strip to go along the curtain header (or top edge), adding an extra 4cm. Press back a 3cm turning along one long edge. Pin the raw edge to the curtain with right sides facing, so that 2cm extends at each end. Machine stitch 1cm from the edge and press the seam up towards the facing.

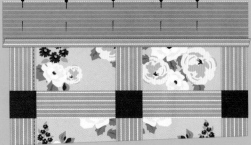

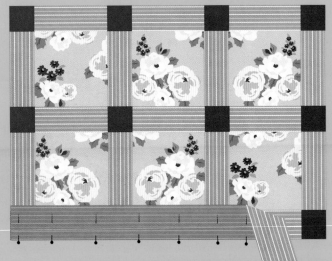

11 Press back the extra fabric in line with the side edges.

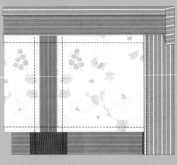

9 Neaten the two side edges in the same way. Cut the facings so that they are 2cm longer than the curtains and sew them on so that this extra fabric extends below the bottom edge. Press it under, in line with the hem, before folding back and sewing down the facings.

12 Press under 1cm at each end of the header tape. Draw out the three gathering cords at at both ends, then pin and stitch the tape to the top of the curtain, so that the top edge lies 2cm down from the fold and the bottom edge conceals the seam.

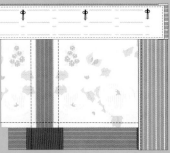

13 Gather the cords to the required width and knot. Insert the curtain hooks and hang in place.

top tip WHEN CUTTING OUT FABRIC WITH A WOVEN (NOT PRINTED) STRIPE, CUT IT FIRST INTO A LONG STRIP, FOLLOWING THE STRIPES, THEN USE A ROTARY CUTTER AND RULER TO TRIM IT INTO RECTANGLES.

Tea Towel Tablecloth

MATERIALS
linen and cotton tea towels
large reel of sewing thread
sewing kit
sewing machine

SKILL LEVEL: 1

When I had a look through my linen cupboard to find a suitable cloth for my new dining table I couldn't find anything that was the right size. However, the neatly folded stacks of linen tea towels, with their unexpected combinations of stripes and checks, gave me an idea... here are the biggest patches in the book!

MEASURING UP
An average tea towel is 40 x 60cm. Instead of getting into any complicated calculations, the best way to work out how many you will need is to gather together all your old tea towels and lay them over the tabletop, allowing a 50cm overhang at each edge!

1 Pick out the smallest tea towel and cut away the hemmed edges and any selvedges. You can do this by following the woven stripes or by drawing guidelines with a fabric marker and a large quilting rule.

2 Trim all the other towels down to the same size, using the small towel as a template. Pin it to each one in turn, centring it over the design, and cut away the margins.

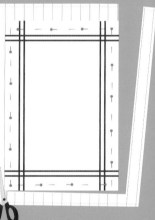

3 Neaten the edge of each towel by machine with a wide zigzag or an overlocking stitch. This will take a while, but it's worth it in the end!

4 Clear the floor and lay out the towels in rows. As with any other patchwork, you should aim for a good balance of colour and pattern, so take time to shuffle them about until you are pleased with the arrangement.

5 Join the horizontal rows along the long edges with a 1.5cm seam. Press all the seams open (this makes the cloth flatter than if they are pressed to one side).

6 Pin the first two rows together along one long edge, matching the seams and corners exactly. Join with a 1.5cm seam and press the seam open. Add the other rows in the same way.

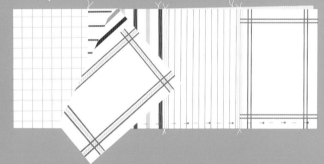

7 Press under a 1.5cm turning around the outside edge of the finished cloth. Mitre each of the corners (see page 21), then pin and machine down the hem 12mm from the fold.

top tip USE A MIXTURE OF OLD AND NEW TEA TOWELS, BUT WASH THEM ALL ON A
HOT SETTING AND PRESS WELL BEFORE STITCHING: THEY MIGHT SHRINK AT DIFFERENT RATES WHICH MAY DISTORT YOUR FINISHED CLOTH.

Sugarbag Doorstop

MATERIALS

scraps of printed canvas or furnishing
  weight fabric
18cm of 2.5cm-wide webbing
20cm of 2cm-wide velcro
plastic beads or 2kg rice for filling
matching sewing thread
sewing kit
sewing machine

CUTTING OUT

from print fabric
twenty-seven 6 x 10cm rectangles
ten 6cm squares
from plain fabric
two 11 x 18cm rectangles for base

SKILL LEVEL: 2

A doorstop is one of those indispensable home accessories that is often overlooked, but there's no reason why it shouldn't be decorative. My patchwork version, in shades of dusky pink, olive and chocolate brown, combines extra large polka dots with furnishing size roses and a tiny floral sprig. It shows how just effective a mixture of fabric with different scale prints can look if you restrict yourself to a limited palette.

The seam allowance is 1cm throughout. Press each seam open after stitching.

1 All four side panels are made in the same way, from five rectangles and two squares. Lay out the patches for the first side as in the drawing. Starting at the bottom, join the two rectangles together. Next, go to the top left and sew the two squares to the adjacent horizontal rectangles. Join these two pieces together horizontally, then add the vertical rectangle to the right edge. Add the two joined ectangles to the bottom edge.

2 Draw a point 1cm in from the top and bottom edges at each corner, to mark the ends of the seam lines.

3 With right sides facing, pin two panels together along one side edge, making sure that they are both the same way up and the seams and corners are aligned. Machine stitch between the dots so that 1cm remains open at each end of the seam. Add the other two panels, then join the remaining sides.

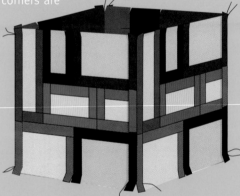

4 The top panel is made from the remaining two squares and seven rectangles, laid out as shown above. Firstly sew the two horizontal rectangles at the bottom together and add a vertical rectangle at each side. Join the two squares to the adjacent rectangles and then sew these two pieces together. Add the vertical rectangle to the right edge, then sew the two halves together.

top tip IF YOU ARE USING RICE AS A FILLING, LINE THE DOORSTOP WITH A LARGE PLASTIC BAG FIRST AND

SEAL THE IT WITH PARCEL TAPE. THIS WAY IT WILL STAY DRY AND THERE'S NO DANGER OF MOULD OR MILDEW.

Sugarbag Doorstop

5 Mark the ends of the seams on the wrong side, as for the side panels.

6 Pin the two ends of the webbing centrally to the sides of the top panel. Machine stitch 5cm from the edge, working two or three rows backwards and forwards to reinforce.

7 With the right side facing downwards pin one edge of the top panel to the top edge of one of the joined side panels. Machine stitch between the dots, working a few backwards stitches to reinforce both ends of the seam. Sew the other three edges in the same way.

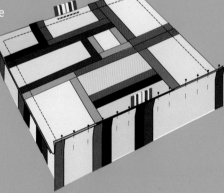

8 Press a 1cm turning over to the right side of one long edge of a base panel. Pin the fuzzy side of the velcro over the turning so that the right edge lies along the fold and machine stitch in place. Press the turning on the other panel to the wrong side and sew the hooked velcro over the turning in the same way.

9 Mark the ends of the seams on the outer corners as for the side panels. Stick the two pieces together, making sure that the top and bottom edges measure 18cm. Sew to the base of the doorstop in the same way as the top panel.

10 Trim a 5mm triangle from the end of each long seam to reduce bulk at the corners.

11 Open up the velcro and turn the door stop right side out. Ease out the seams and corners, then fill the with rice or beads (using a large serving spoon is the least messy way to do this) and close the velcro once again.

---

top tip I WAS LUCKY ENOUGH TO FIND AN ODD LENGTH OF STRIPED WEBBING FOR THE HANDLE, BUT YOU CAN MAKE AN EQUALLY EFFECTIVE ONE FROM A STRIP OF FABRIC FOLLOWING THE INSTRUCTIONS ON PAGE 21.

Tartan Beanbag

SKILL LEVEL: 3

Patchwork isn't all about ditsy floral prints. Larger scale geometrics have a striking, bolder look and I really like the somewhat haphazard effect you get by juxtaposing plaids, tartans and checks. This comfortably squashy beanbag is covered in a combination of three woven fabrics, which started out as cotton picnic blankets. It would make versatile extra seating or a useful footstool, but it's so comfortable that it might just be commandeered by the family pet.

The seam allowance is 1cm throughout. Press each seam open after stitching.

1 To make the side panel, join the patches into three rows, each 180cm long. Pin the side edges together and machine stitch with a 15mm seam. Press the seam allowance to the right and top stitch 3mm from the seam line.

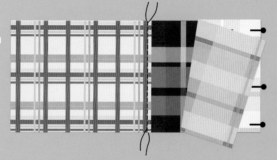

2 With right sides facing, pin the bottom edge of the first strip and the top edge of the second strip together. Machine stitch, again with a 15mm allowance. Join the third strip and press the seam allowances upwards. Top stitch as before.

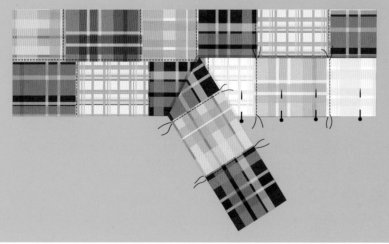

MATERIALS

a minimum of 1m x 50cm each of three plaid fabrics
80 x 70cm plaid for base
0.5 sq m safety standard polystyrene beads in liner
54cm velcro
dressmaker's squared paper
matching sewing thread
sewing machine
sewing kit

CUTTING OUT

from plaid fabrics
Cut the fabrics into 15cm strips, following the woven lines to keep the edges straight. Snip the strips into patches of different widths, ranging from 8 to 20cm wide.
from base plaid fabric
Fold the template along the marked line and use this as a guide to cut two base panels.

TEMPLATE

Make a circle template by drawing onto dressmaker's paper a circle with a 62cm diameter. Draw on a cutting line for the base panel.

top tip YOU COULD USE THIS ONE-OFF PLAID TO REVAMP AN OLD POUFFE OR OTTOMAN... BUT JUST

THINK HOW WONDERFUL A PATCHWORK UPHOLSTERED ARMCHAIR – OR EVEN A SOFA – WOULD LOOK.

Tartan Beanbag

3 Make a similar patchwork panel for the top, from six 75cm rows. Pin on the circle template, lining up the midpoint with the centre seam. Cut out carefully.

4 Join the short edges of the side panel to make a cylinder, and top stitch the seam.

5 Position eight pins around the top edge of the cylinder at intervals of approximately 22cm. Insert eight pins in the outside edge of the circle, 24cm apart.

6 With right sides facing facing, pin the top to the sides, matching up the marker pins first so that they fit together without distortion. Machine stitch all the way round the top, 15mm from the edge.

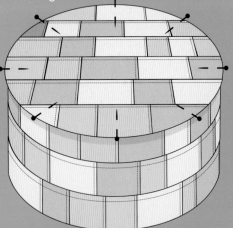

7 Press under a 2cm turning along the straight edge of one base panel. Pull apart the two part of the velcro. Pin the hooked part across the raw edge, 5cm from the fold and with an equal space at each end. Machine stitch around all four sides, 3mm from the edge.

8 Press a 2cm turning back to the right side of the second base panel and sew the other part of the velcro to it in the same way.

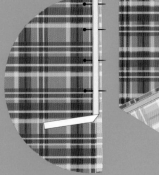

9 Join the two halves of the base by pressing the velcro strips together, but at the same time, slip a sheet of paper between the two parts at the centre so that you can easily separate them later. Pin the slip of paper to the fabric.

10 Join the two halves of the base by pressing the velcro together, but slip a sheet of paper between the two parts at the centre, so that you can easily separate them later. Pin the paper to the fabric.

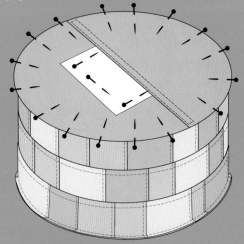

11 Unpin the slip of paper and open out the velcro. Turn right side out and wrestle with the filler until it is inside the cover. You may need to remove some of the beads to make the finished footstool a bit squashier. Close the velcro.

top tip DON'T WORRY TOO MUCH ABOUT THE ORDER IN WHICH YOU ASSEMBLE THE STRIPS – THE COMPLETELY RANDOM ARRANGEMENT OF THE PATTERNS GIVES THIS TYPE OF PATCHWORK ITS INDIVIDUALITY.

Appliqué Tea Towel

MATERIALS
patterned fabric
plain tea towel
15cm spotty ribbon
fusible bonding web
stranded cotyon embroidery thread
sewing thread to match ribbon
sewing kit
iron

SKILL LEVEL: 1

Appliqué is a great way to repurpose some of the odd remnants that textile magpies just can't help hoarding, just like this length of fifties kitchen fabric with nostalgic homemaker imagery. I found the perfect background in a wide linen tea towel with a striped border... but somehow I feel that it might now be more for show than for everyday use.

1 Pick out your favourite prints from the appliqué fabric and cut them out roughly. Following the manufacturer's instructions, fuse them to the adhesive side of the bonding web. Use a sheet of paper towel to protect the iron.

2 Cut each motif out with a curved line, following the contour of the image and leaving a 6–10mm margin of plain fabric all round. Peel off the backing papers.

3 Lay the motifs out on the tea towel, starting with a balanced arrangement of the largest shapes and filling in the gaps with the smaller ones. Using a hot dry iron, press them in position.

4 Edge each motif with a round of blanket stitch, worked with three strands of embroidery thread in a colour to match the background.

5 Make the ribbon into a hanging loop by folding it in half, turning under the ends and stitching it to the top left corner of the tea towel.

top tip THE BLANKET STITCH EDGING GIVES THESE APPLIQUÉ PATCHES A WONDERFUL FINISH, BUT IF TIME AND PATIENCE ARE LIMITED, SIMPLY ANCHOR THEM DOWN WITH A MACHINED ZIGZAG IN CREAM SEWING THREAD.

Hexagon Pincushion

MATERIALS
minimum of 15 x 50cm floral cotton
 fabric
10 x 20cm pink cotton fabric
matching sewing thread
polyester wadding
sewing kit
thick paper for templates

SKILL LEVEL: 2

This simple pincushion design, made up of two hexagon rosettes, has been a starter project for generations of hand stitchers. I have given it a new twist by making the six floral patches identical, so that a new repeating pattern is created when they are joined together. Known to quilt makers as 'fussy cutting', this is a technique that opens up a whole new way of working with fabric and has endless possibilities. Start by making a different design for the front and back and you'll see what I mean!

1 Cut out 14 paper hexagons for the lining papers following the inner outline on page 159. You'll also need to make a window template to help you choose the best floral motifs and to cut accurate matching patches. Trace both outlines, then cut out around them both to make a hexagonal frame.

2 Pick out your favourite self-contained flower motif and place the window template over it. Draw around the outside of the window, then cut out the hexagon.

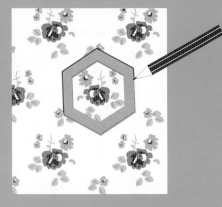

3 Now cut out five more matching floral patches. The easiest way to do this is to pin the original patch precisely over a similar motif then cut around the outside edge.

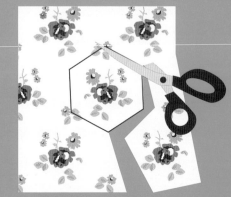

4 Following the outside edge of the window, cut two large pink hexagons for the centre of the rosettes.

5 Pin a template to the centre of a pink hexagon. Working with the template towards you, fold the surplus fabric along one edge forwards and tack it to the paper. Fold the other edges in turn, stitching each one down as you go.

top tip 'FUSSY CUTTING' IS A FASCINATING METHOD, BUT IT CAN TAKE UP A LOT OF FABRIC. CHECK THAT YOU HAVE ENOUGH TO MAKE SIX MATCHING HEXAGONS BEFORE YOU START TO CUT OUT THE PATCHES.

Hexagon Pincushion

6 Cover all the templates in this way then lay them out in the finished order, checking that the flowers within each rosette all face in the same direction.

7 Start by joining the centre to the bottom floral hexagon. Hold the two together with right sides facing, and double check that the innermost edge of the hexagon is at the top. Sew this edge to the pink hexagon with small over stitches, catching a few threads of the fold on each side with every stitch.

8 The next hexagon to the right fits into the angle between these two patches. Check that it is in the right position, then it to the first floral hexagon. Fold in half and sew the next edge to the pink centre. Sew on the other four floral patches in the same way, then make up the second rosette.

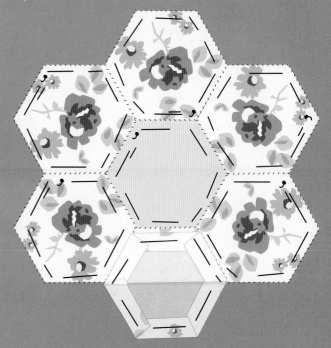

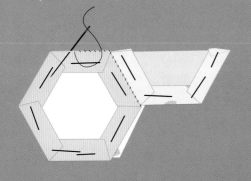

9 Pin the two completed rosettes together with the papers facing inwards and over stitch them together around the outside edge. Leave five hexagon sides unstitched at the bottom edge. Press these edges lightly to set the folds. Unpick all the tacking threads and then remove all the paper templates — this will involve a bit of fiddling about I'm afraid!

10 Stuff the cushion firmly with polyester filling using a pencil to make sure that it reaches right into the corners of the hexagons for a pleasingly plump appearance. Pin the opening and sew four of the edges together. Fill this last space, then slip stitch the final gap.

top tip HONEYCOMB PATCHWORK – A PATTERN MADE UP OF MANY INTERLOCKING HEXAGONS – HAS LONG BEEN

A FAVOURITE TECHNIQUE FOR MAKING QUILTS, SO PERHAPS THIS PROJECT WILL INSPIRE YOU TO KEEP ON STITCHING.

Personalised Dog Bed

MATERIALS
lightweight striped blanket
scraps of suede or felt in fawn, red and brown
red stranded cotton embroidery thread
pencil
90 x 60cm strong canvas
50cm heavy duty zip
matching sewing thread
sewing machine
sewing kit
81 x 56 x 15cm dog bed filler
(http://www.onlineforpets.co.uk/water-resistant-rectangular-dog-cushion-navy-nylon.html)

CUTTING OUT
from blanket fabric
(A) twentyone 18cm squares
(B) three 14 x 18cm rectangles
(C) three 7 x 18cm rectangles
all of the above should have matching stripes
(D) twentyfour 13 x 18cm identical rectangles with a different stripe pattern
from canvas fabric
one 20 x 55cm rectangle
one 63 x 55cm rectangle

TEMPLATE
Stanley, see page 159

SKILL LEVEL: 3

None of my sewing books would be complete without a starring role for Stanley, my beloved Lakeland terrier. So far he has appeared in the guise of a hot water bottle cover, a beanbag and a needlepoint badge, and this time there's even a cuddly toy version of him on pages 100–103. This, however, is the one project that I know he'll really enjoy – a warm, woolly patchwork pet bed!

1 Lay out the six rows of patches in their finished order, following the diagram. The top row starts with a B patch, then has four D patches alternating with three A squares and ends with a narrow C patch. The next row has four D patches alternating with four A squares. These two rows are repeated twice.

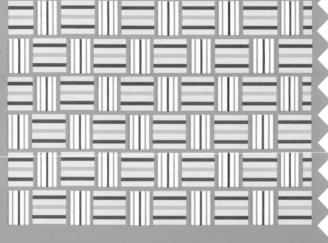

2 Join the patches in each horizontal row with a 1.5cm seam. Press all the seam allowances towards the D patches, then top stitch each seam to strengthen.

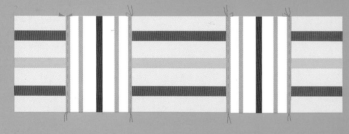

3 Seam the rows together, again with a 1.5cm allowance. Press each allowance downwards and top stitch. Trim a 15cm strip from the top edge, then trim other three edges as necessary to square them off.

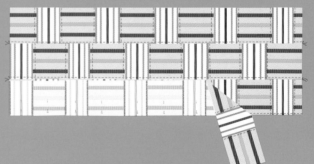

top tip START BY GENTLY LAUNDERING THE BLANKET AND BACKING CANVAS, SO THAT IF YOU EVER NEED TO WASH THE COVER IT WON'T SHRINK ANY FURTHER.

Personalised Dog Bed

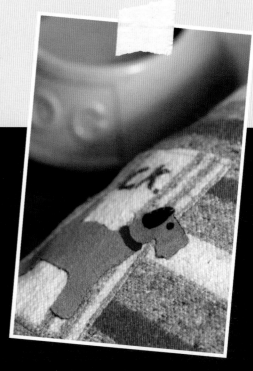

4 The corners are stitched at right angles to give depth to the bed. At each corner in turn, fold and pin the two edges together to make a 45 degree angle. Mark a vertical line 12cm in from the corners. Starting 1.5cm up from the bottom edge, stitch along the marked lines and trim away the excess fabric, 1cm from the seam.

5 Using the full-size template on page 159 cut out a Stanley body from fawn felt or suede, his ear and eye from dark brown and the —collar from red. Pin the body to one bottom corner of the dog bed, 15cm in from the edges, and sew him securely in place with small over stitches. Add the collar, eye and ear. Write your initials – or your dog's name – in the space above and stitch over the letters in chain stitch, using all six strands of the thread.

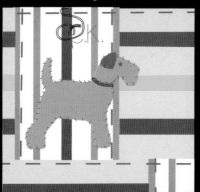

6 Press back a 1cm turning along one 55cm edge of each piece of canvas. Tack these neatened edges to either side of the zip, leaving a 2.5cm gap at each end. Fit a zip foot to your sewing machine and stitch the canvas to the tape, 5mm from the teeth. Tack together the bottom ends of the zip, then open it up.

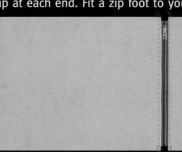

7 With right sides facing, pin the patchwork to the base, opening out the unstitched seam allowance at the corners. The woollen fabric has more 'give' than the canvas, so you will have to ease the edges of the patchwork to fit the base exactly. Machine stitch twice around the outside edge with a 1.5cm seam.

8 Turn right side out, insert the filler pad and do up the zip. The filler is larger than the cover, to give the finished dog bed a well-stuffed, upholstered look.

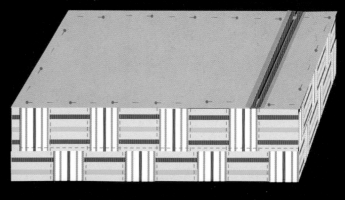

top tip I USED A READY-MADE DOG BED FILLER FROM A SPECIALIST PET SUPPLIER TO GO INSIDE MY COVER, WHICH I CAN EASILY REPLACE WHEN IT BEGINS TO SHOW SIGNS OF WEAR.

Flower Picture

SKILL LEVEL: 2

One of the things that I like best about patchwork and appliqué is fact that you will eventually find the perfect use for every single scrap of fabric... even the very smallest fragments! If you are a hoarder (like me), you're bound to have a stash of offcuts, buttons, threads, beads and ribbons that have been left over from other projects, and this spectacular flower picture is a fantastic way to get creative with them. Look closely and you'll even spot the spare Suffolk puffs from the cashmere cardigan project on page 146.

1 Start by making the crazy patchwork vase. Enlarge the template on page 160 and pin it centrally to the white cotton fabric. Draw round the outside edge and unpin. Fill in the shape with scraps of dress weight prints and shirting, arranging them so the background is covered completely and the fabric overlaps the outline by 2cm all round. Pin down the pieces as you go.

2 Work a row of decorative embroidery over every join, using three strands of cream thread. I chose fly stitch as an alternative to the feather stitch on the Crazy Patch Cushion. You can see how to work both of these on page 29, along with the other stitches I used here: straight stitch, chain stitch and single feather stitch.

3 Using the template as your guide, cut a vase from batting. Pin this centrally to the back of the completed patchwork vase and trim the margin to 1mm all round. Snip into the curves, then turn back the margin around the top and side edges and tack it down.

4 Pin the vase centrally along one long edge of the napkin and slip stitch it in place. Cut a 15cm strip from one long edge of the striped towel, the same length as the napkin. With right sides facing, pin it along the edge of the napkin and over the bottom of the vase. Sew the two together with a 15mm seam, then press the seam towards the stripes.

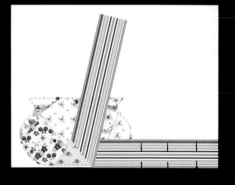

top tip NO TWO APPLIQUÉ PICTURES WILL EVER BE THE SAME, SO USE MY DESIGN AS A SPRINGBOARD FOR YOUR OWN IDEAS. SEARCH THROUGH YOUR TEXTILE COLLECTION AND TAKE INSPIRATION FROM THE FABRICS YOU FIND THERE.

5 Select the prettiest flowers from the furnishing fabric and cut them out roughly. Following the manufacturer's instructions, iron the wrong side onto the bonding web and then cut out neatly around the outside edge of each motif.

6 Draw a few simple leaf shapes on to the paper side of the bonding web and fuse it to the back of the green fabric. Cut them out around the pencil lines. Make four or more Suffolk puffs, as shown on page 147 and using the bonding web, cut circles of fabric to go behind them.

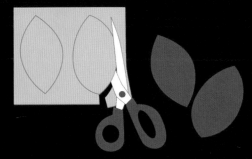

7 Now it's time for some flower arranging. Starting with the largest blooms, position the flowers, leaves, circles and puffs around the vase and shuffle them about until you're pleased with the design. Draw in the curving stems with a dressmaker's pen or chalk pencil, then remove the vase.

8 Peel off the backing papers and press down the flowers, circles and leaves. Slip stitch around the edge of the puffs.

9 Embroider over the stalk lines in green chain stitch and around the edge of the flowers using a variety of stitches to give texture to your picture.

10 Sew the matching buttons in groups of three to fill the spaces between the motifs and add others to the flower centres.

top tip TAKE THIS DESIGN FURTHER BY COMBINING IT WITH MACHINE PATCHWORK. YOU COULD ADD A
DEEP BORDER OF PATCHWORK SQUARES AND USE THE FLOWER BOWL AS THE CENTREPIECE FOR A SMALL QUILT.

Bunny Sweater

MATERIALS

floral print fabric
10cm of 2cm wide ribbon
black and red stranded cotton
  embroidery thread
fusible bonding web
pencil
sewing kit

SKILL LEVEL: 1

Hand knitted garments have a charm all of their own and are so much more appealing than machine made versions. I couldn't resist adding a flowered appliqué rabbit to this tiny v-necked sweater, along with a matching update of the classic elbow patch. The patches are purely decorative, but you could copy the idea if you ever need to cover up any moth holes or areas where the yarn has worn thin.

1 Trace the reversed rabbit template on page 158 and two circles on to the wrong side of the bondaweb and cut out around the outlines. Peel off the backing papers.

2 Position the rabbit centrally on the front of the sweater. Using a cloth to protect the wool from the heat, press it in place with a warm iron. Fuse the circles to the back of the sleeves.

3 Working with three strands of red thread, embroider a round of tailor's buttonhole stitch (see page 29) around the outside edge of each patch. Sew the bunny's eye in black satin stitch, then add three short straight stitches for the whiskers and a satin stitch nose.

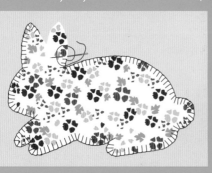

4 To make the bow, cut a 7cm length from the ribbon. Fold it into a loop with the ends at the back. Stitching through all three layers, gather the centre of the ribbon. Fold the remaining piece in half width ways and wrap around the gathered part. Sew the ends securely to the wrong side, then sew the bow to the bunny.

top tip IF YOU PREFER TO USE TRADITIONAL SOFT LEATHER OR SUEDE FOR THE ELBOW PATCHES, YOU WILL

NEED TO STITCH WITH A SPECIAL TRIANGULAR NEEDLE. THIS PIERCES THE LEATHER WITHOUT CAUSING IT TO SPLIT.

Patched Dungarees

MATERIALS
torn garment
scraps of cotton duck or denim
scraps of spot print cotton
small piece of quilt wadding
matching sewing thread
sewing machine

SKILL LEVEL: 1

Here is another example of functional patching, this time on the knees of a pair of toddler-sized dungarees. Once small children start crawling about it's always the knee areas that seem to get the most wear and tear, so these padded racing car patches will cover up the damage as well as providing extra protection. I added the two spot print patches – cut from old handkerchiefs – for a bit of extra pattern and colour.

1 Start by repairing the tear or hole. Undo the poppers at the inside legs and work several closely spaced lines of machine stitch to and fro across the gap. Use the reverse lever to stitch backwards.

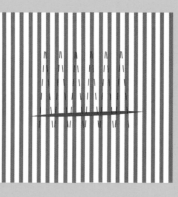

2 Cut two 6cm squares from the spotty fabrics and press under a 5mm turning around each edge of them both. Cut two 12cm squares from the heavier fabric: make them larger if you have a big rip to conceal. From the wadding cut two 11cm squares.

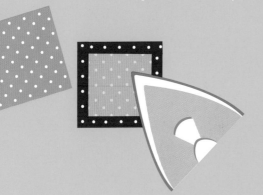

3 The large patches go centrally over the darns and the spotty squares peep out from behind them. Work out the positions, then machine stitch the spotty patches in place with a narrow zigzag in matching thread.

4 Place the wadding in position, then pin the large patches down over them. Rethread the sewing machine with a colour to match, then zigzag down.

top tip WHEN YOU ARE MAKING A REPAIR PATCH, MAKE SURE THAT IT IS A SIMILAR WEIGHT TO THE GARMENT.

I USED COTTON DUCK ON THESE CANVAS DUNGAREES, BUT DENIM WOULD HAVE WORKED JUST AS WELL.

Puff Collar Cardigan

MATERIALS

cardigan
selection of print fabrics – about 12cm
  square for each puff
pair of compasses and paper
self-cover buttons
matching sewing thread
sewing kit

SKILL LEVEL: 1

When I was planning the square cushion cover on page 88, all of the Suffolk Puffs were randomly strewn across my desk. I loved the mixture of fabrics and the way they overlapped, so started wondering whether there was another – slightly less formal – way in which I could use these pretty little patches. I came up with the idea of embellishing a cashmere cardigan with a 'collar' of puffs... great to wear over a summery floral tea dress. Turn to page 148 to see what I did next!

1 Cut an 11cm diameter disc of paper to use as your template. Using this as a guide, cut about 35 circles from the various fabrics and make them up into Suffolk Puffs, as shown on page 89.

2 Pin a row of puffs all the way around the neckline, at front and back, then arrange the rest on either side of the front to create a symmetrical collar shape. Overlap the edges of a few, then pin them all in place. Depending on the size and shape of your cardigan, you may find you need to make a couple more puffs to fill all the spaces.

3 Sew each puff down with a round of small straight stitches in matching thread. You'll need to stitch through all the layers where the puffs overlap.

4 It's the details that make things really special, so I as a finishing touch I replaced the basic buttons on this cardigan with small, round self-cover buttons, made from the foral fabric offcuts. The button kits provide all the instructions for how to do this.

top tip CHOOSE A NARROW COLOUR PALETTE TO COMPLEMENT YOUR CARDIGAN. I USED STRIPES, SPOTS AND GINGHAM IN SHADES OF PINK AND RED, THEN ADDED A SPRINKLING OF PUFFS IN A CO-ORDINATING FLOWERED DRESS FABRIC.

Puff Necklace

MATERIALS
scraps of plain and floral print
 dress-weight fabric
matching sewing thread
one long or two short chain necklaces
masking tape
sewing kit

CUTTING OUT
from floral print fabric
one 12cm circle
two 10cm circles
two 8cm circles
from plain fabric
two 12cm circles
two 8cm circles

TEMPLATES
8cm, 10cm and 12cm diameter circles

SKILL LEVEL: 1

Last but not least, is this sweet puff necklace – the ideal accessory to wear with your favourite floaty summer frock, or over a plain sweater. Offcuts of viscose crepe were used, which gives the puffs an especially three-dimensional aspect, but it would look just as good in any floral print with a toning plain fabric.

1 Make all the circles of fabric into puffs, as for the cushion cover on page 89. Lay them out in decreasing size to form a horseshoe shape, with the largest floral puff at the centre.

2 Pin the puffs to each other where they overlap, keeping them in the same formation. Sew them together with small stab stitches, sewing through all the layers of fabric.

3 Turn the puffs over and place the chain centrally across the back, following the curve. Secure it in place with short lengths of masking tape, then sew the chain to the back of the puffs.

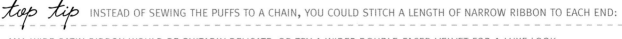

top tip INSTEAD OF SEWING THE PUFFS TO A CHAIN, YOU COULD STITCH A LENGTH OF NARROW RIBBON TO EACH END: 3MM-WIDE SATIN RIBBON WOULD BE SUITABLY DELICATE, OR TRY A WIDER DOUBLE-FACED VELVET FOR A LUXE LOOK.

Useful Addresses

Patchwork shops

The Bramble Patch
West Street
Weedon
Northamptonshire NN7 4QU
01327 342121
www.thebramblepatch.co.uk

Coast & Country Crafts & Quilts
Barras Moor Farm
Perranarworthal, Truro
Cornwall TR3 7PE
01872 870478
www.coastandcountrycrafts.co.uk

The Cotton Patch
1285 Stratford Road
Hall Green
Birmingham B28 9AJ
0121 7022840
www.cottonpatch.net

Creative Quilting
32 Bridge Road
Hampton Court Village
East Molesey
Surrey KT8 9HA
020 8941 7075
www.creativequilting.co.uk

The Fat Quarters
5 Chopwell Road
Blackhall Mill
Newcastle Upon Tyne NE17 7TN
01207 565728
www.thefatquarters.co.uk

Heirs & Graces
Wesleyan House
Dale Road
Darley Dale
Derbyshire DE4 2HX
01629 734100
www.patchworkdirect.com

Patch – Fabric and Haberdashery
9 Bevan Street East
Lowestoft
Suffolk NR32 2AA
01502 588778
www.patchfabrics.co.uk

Patchwork Garden
630 Abbeydale Road
Sheffield
South Yorkshire S7 2BA
0114 258 3763
www.patchworkgarden.co.uk

Pelenna Patchworks
5 Bevans Terrace
Pontrhydyfen
Port Talbot
West Glamorgan SA12 9TR
01639 898444
www.pelennapatchworks.co.uk

Quilter's Haven
68 High Street
Wickham Market
Woodbridge
Suffolk IP13 0QU
01728 746275
www.quilters-haven.co.uk

Tikki
293 Sandycombe Road
Kew
Surrey TW9 3LU
020 8948 8462
www.tikkilondon.com

Fabric and haberdashery shops

Bedecked
5 Castle Street
Hay-on-Wye
Hereford HR3 5DF
01497 822769
www.bedecked.co.uk

Cloth House
47 Berwick Street
London W1F 8SJ
020 7437 5155
www.clothhouse.net

Design-a-Cushions
74 Drum Brae South
Edinburgh EH12 8TH
0131 539 0080
www.deisgn-a-cushions.co.uk

Harts of Hertford
14 Bull Plain
Hertford SG14 1DT
01992 558106
www.hartsofhertford.com

John Lewis
Oxford Street
London W1A 1EX
and branches nationwide
08456 049049
www.johnlewis.com

MacCulloch & Wallis
25–26 Dering Street
London W1S 1AT
020 7629 0311
www.macculloch-wallis.co.uk

The Makery Emporium
16 Northumberland Place
Bath
Avon BA1 5AR
01225 487708
www.themakeryonline.co.uk

Mandors
134 Renfrew Street
Glasgow G3 6ST
0141 332 7716
www.mandors.co.uk

Merrick & Day
Redbourne Road
Redbourne
Gainsborough
Lincolnshire DN21 4TG
01652 648 814
www.merrick-day.com

Millie Moon
20 Paul Street
Frome
Somerset BA11 1DT
01373 464650
www.milliemoonshop.co.uk

Our Patterned Hand
49 Broadway Market
London E8 4PH
020 7812 9912
www.ourpatternedhand.co.uk

Rags
19 Chapel Walk
Crowngate Shopping Centre
Worcester WR1 3LD
01905 612330

Sew and So's
14 Upper Olland Street
Bungay
Suffolk NR35 1BG
01986 896147
www.sewandsos.co.uk

Patchwork and sewing classes

Heatherlea Design
01332 661562
www.heatherleadesign.com

Just Between Friends
44 Station Way
Buckhurst Hill
Essex IG9 6LN
020 8502 9191
www.justbetweenfriends.co.uk

Liberty Sewing School
Regent Street
London W1B 5AH
www.liberty.co.uk

The Makery
146 Walcot Street
Bath
Avon BA1 5BL
01225 421175
www.themakeryonline.co.uk

Sew Over It
78 Landor Road
Clapham North
London SW9 9PH
020 7326 0376
www.sewoverit.co.uk

The Thrifty Stitcher
Unit 21
4–6 Shelford Place
Stoke Newington
London N16 9HS
07779 255087
www.thethriftystitcher.co.uk

Modern Approach Sewing School
Astra Business Centre
Roman Way
Ribbleton
Preston PR2 5AP
01772 498862
www.sewjanetmoville.co.uk

Sue Hazell Sewing Tuition
Southcombe House
Chipping Norton
Oxfordshire OX7 5QH
www.sewing-tuition.co.uk

The Studio London
Studio 5
Trinity Buoy Wharf
64 Orchard Place
London E14 0JW
www.thestudiolondon.co.uk

Cath Kidston stores

Bath
3 Broad Street
Milsom Place
Bath BA1 5LJ
01225 331 006

Brighton
31a & 32 East Street
Brighton BN1 1HL
01273 227 420

Bristol
79 Park Street
Clifton
Bristol BS1 5PF
0117 930 4722

Cambridge
31 Market Hill
Cambridge CB2 3NU
01223 351 810

Cheltenham
21 The Promenade
Cheltenham GL50 1LE
01242 245 912

Chichester
24 South Street
Chichester PO19 1EL
01243 850 100

Dublin
Unit CSD 1.3
Dundrum Shopping Centre
Dublin 16
01 296 4430

Edinburgh
58 George Street
Edinburgh EH2 2LR
0131 220 1509

Guildford
14–18 Chertsey Street
Guildford GU1 4HD
01483 564 798

Harrogate
4–6 James Street
Harrogate HG1 1RF
01423 531 481

Kildare
Unit 21c Kildare Village
Nurney Road
Kildare Town
00 353 45 535 084

Kingston
10 Thames Street
Kingston Upon Thames KT1 1PE
020 8546 6760

Leeds
26 Lands Lane
Leeds LS1 6LB
0113 397 1330

Liverpool
18 School Lane
Liverpool L1 3BT
0151 709 2747

London – Battersea
142 Northcote Road
Battersea
London SW11 6RD
020 7228 6571

London – Chiswick
125 Chiswick High Road
Chiswick
London W4 2ED
020 8995 8052

London – Covent Garden
28–32 Shelton Street
Covent Garden
London WC2H 9JE
020 7836 4803

London – Fulham
668 Fulham Road
Fulham
London SW6 5RX
020 7731 6531

London – Heathrow Terminal 4
Departure Lounge
Heathrow Airport
Hounslow TW6 3XA
020 8759 5578

London – Kings Road
322 Kings Road
Chelsea
London SW3 5UH
020 7351 7335

London – Marylebone
51 Marylebone High Street
Marylebone
London W1U 5HW
020 7935 6555

London – Notting Hill
158 Portobello Road
Notting Hill
London W11 2BE
020 7727 5278

London – Sloane Square
27 Kings Road
Chelsea
London SW3 4RP
020 3463 4840

Marlow
6 Market Square
Marlow SL7 1DA
01628 484 443

Oxford
6 Broad Street
Oxford OX1 3AJ
01865 791 576

Portsmouth
Gunwharf Quays
Portsmouth PO1 3TU
02392 832 982

St Ives
67 Fore Street
St Ives TR26 1HE
01736 798 001

Tunbridge Wells
59–61 High Street
Tunbridge Wells TN1 1XU
01892 521 197

Wimbledon Village
3 High Street
Wimbledon SW19 5DX
020 8944 1001

Winchester
46 High Street
Winchester SO23 9BT
01962 870 620

Windsor
24 High Street
Windsor SL4 1LH
01753 830 591

York
32 Stonegate
York YO1 8AS
01904 733 653

Concessions in:
Bicester Village (outlet store),
Oxfordshire
Fenwicks, Northumberland Street,
Newcastle Upon Tyne
Selfridges, The Bull Ring, Birmingham
Selfridges, Oxford Street, London
Selfridges, Exchange Square, Manchester
Selfridges, Trafford Centre, Manchester

For up-to-date information on all
Cath Kidston stores, please visit
www.cathkidston.co.uk

Acknowledgements

My special thanks to everyone involved in the creation of this book: to Elaine Ashton and Jessica Pemberton, to Lucinda Ganderton and her assistant Lis Gunner for the making of the projects, to Pia Tryde for her inspiring photography, and to Anne Furniss, Helen Lewis, Lisa Pendreigh and Katherine Case at Quadrille.

Cath Kidston

Series Creative Coordinator:
Elaine Ashton
Design Assistant to Cath Kidston:
Jessica Pemberton
Patchwork Coordinator and Consultant:
Lucinda Ganderton
Patchwork Assistant: Lis Gunner

Editorial Director: Anne Furniss
Art Director: Helen Lewis
Project Editor: Lisa Pendreigh
Designer: Katherine Case
Photographer: Pia Tryde
Illustrators: Bridget Bodoano and Joy FitzSimmons
Production Director: Vincent Smith
Production Controller: Aysun Hughes

If you have any comments or queries regarding the instructions in this book, please contact us at enquiries@quadrille.co.uk.

First published in 2011 by
Quadrille Publishing Limited
Alhambra House
27–31 Charing Cross Road
London WC2H 0LS

Cataloguing-in-Publication Data: a catalogue record for this book is available from the British Library.

ISBN 978 184400 988 6

Templates

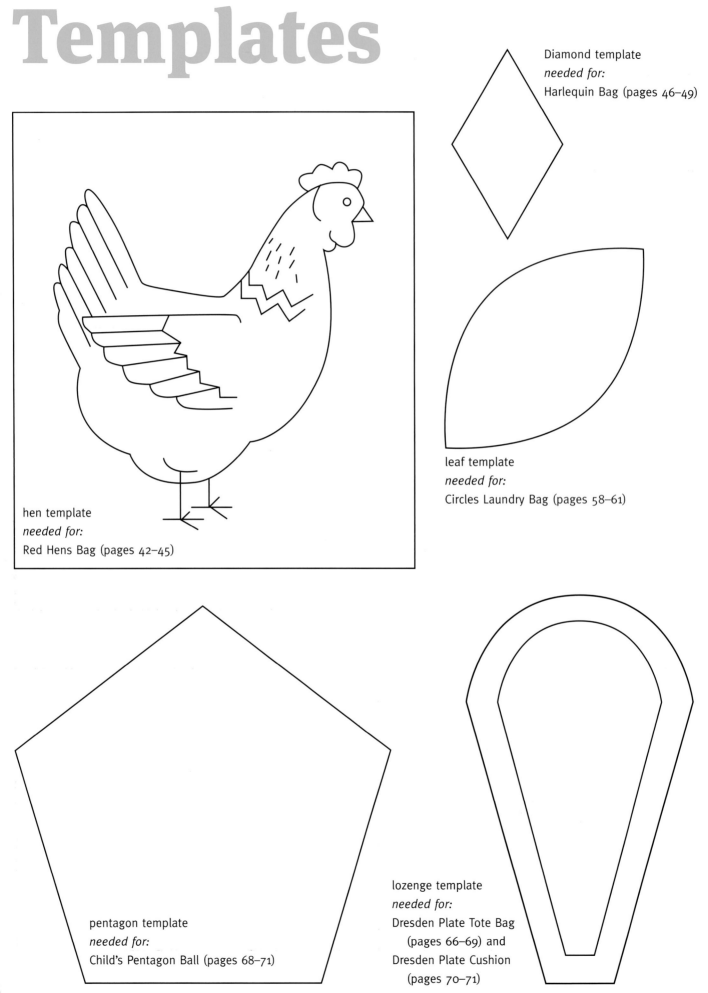

Diamond template
needed for:
Harlequin Bag (pages 46–49)

leaf template
needed for:
Circles Laundry Bag (pages 58–61)

hen template
needed for:
Red Hens Bag (pages 42–45)

pentagon template
needed for:
Child's Pentagon Ball (pages 68–71)

lozenge template
needed for:
Dresden Plate Tote Bag
(pages 66–69) and
Dresden Plate Cushion
(pages 70–71)

Stanley's ear, nose, square, rectangle and triangle templates
needed for:
Stanley Toy (pages 100–103)

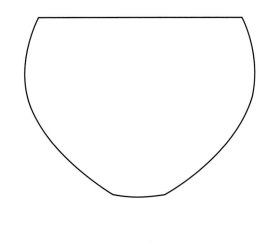

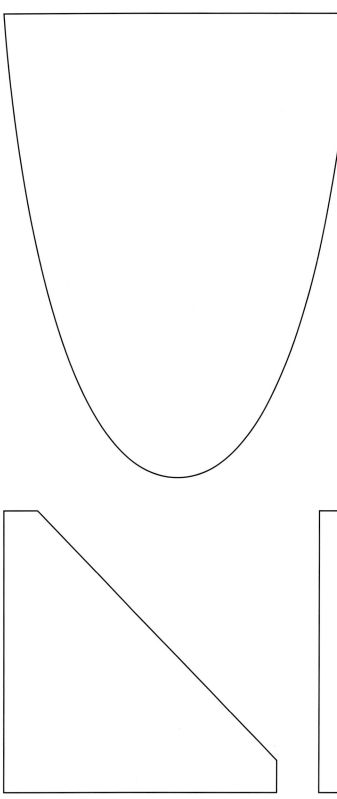

bunny and circle templates
needed for:
Bunny Sweater (pages 106–107)

bunny template
needed for:
Bunny Blanket (pages 104–105)

star point and octogon templates
needed for:
Star Throw (pages 106–109)

hexagon templates
needed for:
Hexagon Pincushion (pages 130–133)

Stanley's body, ear, eye and collar templates
needed for:
Personalised Dog Bed (pages 134–137)

vase template
needed for:
Flower Picture (pages 138–141)

*The Illustrated Favourite Poems
We Learned at School*

First published in 1997 by Mercier Press 16 Hume Street Dublin 2 and PO Box 5 5 French Church Street Cork
Trade enquiries to CMD Distribution 55A Spruce Avenue Stillorgan Industrial Park Blackrock County Dublin
Tel: (01) 294 2556; Fax: (01) 294 2560

Published in the US and Canada by the Irish American Book Company, 6309 Monarch Park Place, Niwot, Colorado, 80503
Tel: (303) 652-2710, (800) 452-7115 ; Fax: (303) 652-2689, (800) 401-9705

10 9 8 7 6 5 4 3

A CIP record for this title is available from the British Library

Cover design by Penhouse Design from a photograph courtesy of Mary Feehan
Set by Richard Parfrey
Printed in Ireland by Betaprint Newtown Industrial Estate Clonshaugh Dublin 17

ACKNOWLEDGEMENTS: POETRY
For permission to reproduce copyright material, the editor and publishers are grateful to the following:
Sairséal Ó Marcaigh for 'Cúl an Tí' from *Scáthán Véarsaí* by Seán Ó Ríordáin; the executors of the Katharine Tynan estate for 'Sheep and Lambs'; Simon D. Campbell for Joseph Campbell's 'I Will Go with My Father'; Douglas Sealy for 'An gleann 'nar tógadh mé' by Dúghlas de Híde; the executors of the W. H. Davies estate and Jonathan Cape for 'Lesiure' from *The Complete Poems of W. H. Davies*; Máire Mhac an tSaoi for 'Tháinig long ó Valparaiso' by Monsignor Pádraig de Brún; the literary trustees of Walter de la Mare and the Society of Authors as their representative for 'The Listeners' from *The Complete Poems of Walter de la Mare*; the Society of Authors as the Literary Representative of the Estate of John Masefield for 'Sea-fever'; Devin-Adair Publishers Inc. for 'The Old Woman of the Roads' and 'Cradle Song' by Padraic Colum.
Every attempt has been made to get in touch with copyright holders. The publishers will be glad to come to a suitable arrangement with any copyright holders whom it has not been possible to reach.

ACKNOWLEDGEMENTS: PHOTOGRAPHS
Father Browne SJ Collection: p. 11 (Ploughing at Maguire's Bridge, 1930); p. 33 ('Little Gaels' at Carrowcarew, near Maam, County Galway, 1925); p. 53 (Maureen Phelan at Straffan, County Kildare, 1925)
Anthony Barry, *No Lovelier City: a Portrait of Cork* (1995): pp. 13; 93
Photographs reproduced with the kind permission of the Trustees of the Ulster Museum, Belfast: pp. 15; 27 (Swift Collection); 45 (Bigger Collection); 47, 51 (Bert Martin Collection); 59; 63 (Bigger Collection); 67 (Bert Martin Collection); 85; 99 (Bert Martin Collection)
Ulster Folk and Transport Museum: pp. 29 (Everton Public Elementary School Choir: The *Belfast Telegraph*); 65; 95; 103, 107 (WAG Collection)
Public Record Office of Northern Ireland (Alice Mary Young Collection): pp. 17; 21; 23; 39; 61; 71; 81; 83
Colman Doyle: pp. 77; 91
Hulton Getty Picture Library: p. 35
Thomas F. Walsh (family photographs): pp. 43; 49; 57; 97
Willy Kelly: pp. 19 (Cork 1979); 37 (Kerry 1976); 87 (Kerry 1976)
Richard Parfrey: p. 73

The Illustrated Favourite Poems
We Learned at School

Thomas F. Walsh

MERCIER PRESS

Contents

Introduction

It is now almost five years since I first collected *Favourite Poems We Learned in School*. It was such a success that *More Favourite Poems We Learned in School* and *Favourite Poems We Learned in School as Gaeilge* quickly followed. These collections continue to be enjoyed by thousands of readers both here in Ireland and abroad.

The success of these collections of old school poems has borne out my belief that most of us really like poetry and that we especially like to remember the powerful, haunting and musical lines from the days of our childhood when we first encountered them in school and committed them to memory.

Little did we realise then that there would come a time when we would treasure these old school poems, when we would mourn their passing out of reach and regret the fact that we had all but forgotten them, except, perhaps, for a fragment of a line.

We should never underestimate the emotive and nostalgic power of poetry, how it can echo in the memory and carry us back to the days of innocence and wonder. I have received many letters from people all over the world telling me how much they enjoyed those abiding gems from their old schoolbooks.

Here is a collection of what you might call the very best of the *Favourite Poems*, the ones that have proved to be the most popular and enduring. These are the poems that have appeared most often in schoolbooks over the years. I'm sure you will enjoy them.

A photograph is a bit like an old poem; it captures a flicker of life and stirs the emotions: it conquers time in a moment. The beautiful photographs in this volume carry us back, like the old poems, to our schooldays – when we lived in a very different world. They are photographs of the children we were, the places we lived in, the countryside and streets we knew before time moved on.

I am very grateful to the keepers of the great photographic collections – notably the Father Francis Browne SJ Collection, the Ulster Museum and the Ulster Folk and Transport Museum – for permission to reproduce their photographs. Thanks especially to Pat McClean and Vivienne Pollock of the Ulster Museum for their help and enthusiasm, and also to Willy Kelly and Richard Parfrey for allowing us to use their photographs.

Thomas F. Walsh, October 1997

I Will Go with My Father

I will go with my father a-ploughing
To the green field by the sea,
And the rooks and the crows and the seagulls
Will come flocking after me.
I will sing to the patient horses
With the lark in the white of the air,
And my father will sing the plough-song
That blesses the cleaving share.

I will go with my father a-sowing
To the red field by the sea,
And the rooks and the gulls and the starlings
Will come flocking after me.
I will sing to the striding sowers
With the finch on the flowering sloe,
And my father will sing the seed-song
That only the wise men know.

I will go with my father a-reaping
To the brown field by the sea,
And the geese and the crows and the children
Will come flocking after me.
I will sing to the weary reapers
With the wren in the heat of the sun,
And my father will sing the scythe-song
That joys for the harvest done.

Joseph Campbell (1879–1944)

A Noble Boy

The woman was old, and feeble, and grey,
And bent with the chill of the winter's day;
The street was wet with the recent snow,
And the woman's feet were weary and slow.
She stood at the crossing, and waited long,
Alone, uncared for, amid the throng.
Down the street, with laughter and shout,
Glad in the freedom of 'school let out',
Came the boys, like a flock of sheep;
Hailing the snow, piled white and deep.
Past the woman, so old and grey,
Hastened the children on their way,
Nor offered a helping hand to her,
So meek, so timid, afraid to stir.

At last came one of the merry troop –
The gayest boy of all the group;
He paused beside her, and whispered low,
'I'll help you across if you wish to go';
He guided the trembling feet along,
Proud, that his own were firm and strong.
Then back again to his friends, he went,
His young heart happy, and well content,
'She is somebody's mother, boys, you know,
Although she is old, and poor and slow.
And I hope some fellow will lend a hand
To help my mother – you understand –
If e'er she be poor, and old and grey,
When her own dear boy is far away.'

And 'somebody's mother' bowed low her head,
In her home that night, and the prayer she said
Was, 'God be kind to the noble boy,
Who is somebody's son, and pride, and joy.'

Mary Dow Brine (fl. 1878)

A Cradle Song

O men from the fields!
Come gently within.
Tread softly, softly,
O men coming in.

Mavourneen is going
From me and from you,
Where Mary will fold him
With mantle of blue!

From reek of the smoke
And cold of the floor,
And the peering of things
Across the half-door.

O men from the fields!
Soft, softly come thro'.
Mary puts round him
Her mantle of blue.

Padraic Colum (1881–1972)

Four Ducks on a Pond

Four ducks on a pond,
A grass-bank beyond,
A blue sky of spring,
White clouds on the wing:
What a little thing
To remember for years –
To remember with tears!

William Allingham (1824–89)

Farewell to the Farm

The coach is at the door at last;
The eager children, mounting fast
And kissing hands, in chorus sing:
Goodbye, goodbye to everything!

To house and garden, field and lawn,
To meadow-gates we swung upon,
To pump and stable, tree and swing,
Goodbye, goodbye to everything!

And fare you well for evermore,
O ladder at the hayloft door,
O hayloft where the cobwebs cling,
Goodbye, goodbye to everything!

Crack goes the whip, and off we go;
The trees and houses smaller grow;
Last, round the woody turn we swing:
Goodbye, goodbye to everything!

Robert Louis Stevenson (1850–94)

All Things Bright and Beautiful

All things bright and beautiful,
All creatures great and small,
All things wise and wonderful,
The Lord God made them all.

Each little flower that opens,
Each little bird that sings,
He made their glowing colours,
He made their tiny wings.

The rich man in his castle,
The poor man at his gate,
God made them high or lowly,
And ordered their estate.

The purple-headed mountain,
The river running by,
The sunset and the morning,
That brightens up the sky;

The cold wind in the winter,
The pleasant summer sun,
The ripe fruits in the garden –
He made them every one.

The tall trees in the greenwood,
The meadows for our play,
The rushes by the water
To gather every day;

He gave us eyes to see them,
And lips that we might tell,
How great is God Almighty,
Who has made all things well.

Cecil Frances Alexander (1818–95)

The Presence of God

I see His blood upon the rose,
And in the stars the glory of His eyes;
His body gleams amid eternal snows,
His tears fall from the skies.

I see His face in every flower;
The thunder, and the singing of the birds
Are but His voice; and, carven by His power,
Rocks are His written words.

All pathways by His feet are worn;
His strong heart stirs the ever-beating sea;
His crown of thorns is twined with every thorn;
His cross is every tree.

Joseph Mary Plunkett (1887–1916)

To Autumn

Season of mists and mellow fruitfulness,
Close bosom-friend of the maturing sun;
Conspiring with him how to load and bless
With fruit the vines that round the thatch-eaves run,
To bend with apples the mossed cottage trees,
And fill all fruit with ripeness to the core;
To swell the gourd, and plump the hazel shells
With a sweet kernel; to set budding more,
And still more, later flowers for the bees,
Until they think warm days will never cease;
For Summer has o'erbrimmed their clammy cells.

Who hath not seen thee oft amid thy store?
Sometimes whoever seeks abroad may find
Thee sitting careless on a granary floor,
Thy hair soft-lifted by the winnowing wind;
Or on a half-reaped furrow sound asleep,
Drowsed with the fume of poppies, while thy hook
Spares the next swath and all its twined flowers:
And sometimes like a gleaner thou dost keep
Steady thy laden head across a brook;
Or by a cyder-press, with patient look,
Thou watchest the last oozings, hours by hours.

Where are the songs of Spring? Ay, where are they?
Think not of them, thou hast thy music too –
While barrèd clouds bloom the soft-dying day
And touch the stubble-plains with rosy hue;
Then in a wailful choir the small gnats mourn
Among the river sallows, borne aloft
Or sinking as the light wind lives or dies;
And full-grown lambs loud bleat from hilly bourn;
Hedge-crickets sing; and now with treble soft
The red-breast whistles from a garden croft,
And gathering swallows twitter in the skies.

John Keats (1795–1821)

Trees

I think that I shall never see
A poem lovely as a tree.

A tree whose hungry mouth is prest
Against the earth's sweet flowing breast;

A tree that looks at God all day,
And lifts her leafy arms to pray;

A tree that may in Summer wear
A nest of robins in her hair;

Upon whose bosom snow has lain;
Who intimately lives with rain.

Poems were made by fools like me,
But only God can make a tree.

Joyce Kilmer (1886–1918)

Sheep and Lambs

All in the April evening,
April airs were abroad;
The sheep with their little lambs
Passed me by on the road.

The sheep with their little lambs
Passed me by on the road;
All in the April evening,
I thought on the Lamb of God.

The lambs were weary, and crying
With a weak, human cry.
I thought on the Lamb of God
Going meekly to die.

Up in the blue, blue mountains
Dewy pastures are sweet;
Rest for the little bodies,
Rest for the little feet.

But for the Lamb of God,
Up on the hill-top green,
Only a cross of shame,
Two stark crosses between.

All in the April evening,
April airs were abroad;
I saw the sheep with their lambs,
And thought on the Lamb of God.

Katharine Tynan (1861–1931)

Hy-Brazil – the Isle of the Blest

On the ocean that hollows the rocks where ye dwell,
A shadowy land has appear'd as they tell;
Men thought it a region of sunshine and rest,
And they call'd it 'O Brazil – the Isle of the Blest'.
From year unto year, on the ocean's blue rim,
The beautiful spectre show'd lovely and dim;
The golden clouds curtain'd the deep where it lay.
And it look'd like an Eden, away, far away.

A peasant, who heard of the wonderful tale,
In the breeze of the Orient loosen'd his sail;
From Ara, the holy, he turn'd to the west,
For though Ara was holy, O'Brazil was blest.
He heard not the voices that call'd from the shore –
He heard not the rising wind's menacing roar:
Home, kindred, and safety he left on that day,
And he sped to O'Brazil, away, far away!

Morn rose on the deep, and that shadowy Isle
O'er the faint rim of distance reflected its smile;
Noon burn'd on the wave, and that shadowy shore
Seem'd lovelily distant, and faint as before:
Lone evening came down on the wanderer's track,
And to Ara again he look'd timidly back;
Oh! far on the verge of the ocean it lay,
Yet the Isle of the Blest was away, far away!

Rash dreamer, return! O ye winds of the main,
Bear him back to his old peaceful Ara again!
Rash fool! for a vision of fanciful bliss
To barter the calm life of labour and peace!
The warning of reason was spoken in vain,
He never revisited Ara again;
Night fell on the deep, amidst tempest and spray,
And he died on the waters, away, far away!

To you, gentle friends, need I pause to reveal
The lessons of prudence my verses conceal;
How the phantom of pleasure seen distant in youth,
Oft lures a weak heart from the circle of truth.
All lovely it seems, like that shadowy isle,
And the eye of the wisest is caught by its smile;
But ah! for the heart it has tempted to stray
From the sweet home of duty, away, far away!

Poor friendless adventurer! vainly might he
Look back to green Ara along the wild sea;
But the wanderer's heart has a Guardian above,
Who, though erring, remembers the child of His love.
Oh, who at the proffer of safety would spurn,
When all that He asks is the will to return;
To follow a phantom, from day unto day,
And die in the tempest, away, far away!

Gerald Griffin (1803–40)

The Wayfarer

The beauty of the world hath made me sad,
This beauty that will pass;
Sometimes my heart hath shaken with great joy
To see a leaping squirrel in a tree,
Or a red lady-bird upon a stalk
Or little rabbits in a field at evening,
Lit by a slanting sun,
Or some green hill where shadows drifted by,
Some quiet hill where mountainy men hath sown
And soon would reap, near to the gate of Heaven;
Or children with bare feet upon the sands
Of some ebbed sea, or playing on the streets
Of little towns in Connacht,
Things young and happy.
And then my heart hath told me:
These will pass,
Will pass and change, will die and be no more,
Things bright and green, things young and happy;
And I have gone upon my way
Sorrowful.

Padraic H. Pearse (1879–1916)

The Old Woman of the Roads

O to have a little house!
To own the hearth and stool and all!
The heaped-up sods upon the fire,
The pile of turf against the wall!

To have a clock with weights and chains,
And pendulum swinging up and down!
A dresser filled with shining delph,
Speckled with white and blue and brown!

I could be busy all the day
Cleaning and sweeping hearth and floor,
And fixing on their shelf again
My white and blue and speckled store!

I could be quiet there at night
Beside the fire and by myself,
Sure of a bed and loath to leave
The ticking clock and the shining delph!

Och! but I'm weary of mist and dark,
And roads where there's never a house nor bush,
And tired I am of bog and road,
And the crying wind and the lonesome hush!

And I am praying to God on high,
And I am praying Him night and day,
For a little house – a house of my own –
Out of the wind and the rain's way.

Padraic Colum (1881–1972)

Nature's Child

Still south I went, and west, and south again,
Through Wicklow from the morning to the night,
And far from cities and the sights of men,
Lived with the sunshine and the moon's delight.

I knew the stars, the flowers and the birds,
The grey and wintry sides of many glens,
And did but half remember human words,
In converse with the mountains, moors and fens.

J. M. Synge (1871–1909)

Lament for Thomas MacDonagh

He shall not hear the bittern cry
In the wild sky, where he is lain,
Nor voices of the sweeter birds
Above the wailing of the rain.

Nor shall he know when loud March blows
Thro' slanting snows her fanfare shrill,
Blowing to flame the golden cup
Of many an upset daffodil.

But when the Dark Cow leaves the moor
And pastures poor with greedy weeds
Perhaps he'll hear her low at morn,
Lifting her horn in pleasant meads.

Francis Ledwidge (1891–1917)

The Burial of Sir John Moore

Not a drum was heard, not a funeral note,
As his corse to the ramparts we hurried;
Not a soldier discharged his farewell shot
O'er the grave where our hero we buried.

We buried him darkly at dead of night,
The sods with our bayonets turning;
By the struggling moonbeam's misty light
And the lantern dimly burning.

No useless coffin enclosed his breast,
Not in sheet nor in shroud we wound him;
But he lay like a warrior taking his rest,
With his martial cloak around him.

Few and short were the prayers we said,
And we spoke not a word of sorrow;
But we steadfastly gazed on the face that was dead,
And we bitterly thought of the morrow.

We thought as we hollow'd his narrow bed
And smoothed down his lonely pillow,
That the foe and the stranger would tread o'er his head,
And we far away on the billow!

Lightly they'll talk of the spirit that's gone
And o'er his cold ashes upbraid him –
But little he'll reck, if they let him sleep on
In the grave where a Briton has laid him.

But half of our heavy task was done
When the clock struck the hour for retiring:
And we heard the distant and random gun
That the foe was sullenly firing.

Slowly and sadly we laid him down,
From the field of his fame fresh and gory;
We carved not a line, and we raised not a stone,
But we left him alone with his glory.

Charles Wolfe (1791–1823)

The March to Kinsale

O'er many a river bridged with ice,
Through many a vale with snow-drifts dumb,
Past quaking fen and precipice
The Princes of the North are come!

Lo, these are they that year by year
Roll'd back the tide of England's war; –
Rejoice, Kinsale! thy help is near!
That wondrous winter march is o'er.

And thus they sang, 'Tomorrow morn
Our eyes shall rest upon the foe:
Roll on, swift night, in silence borne,
And blow, thou breeze of sunrise, blow!'

Blithe as a boy on marched the host,
With droning pipe and clear-voiced harp;
At last above that southern coast
Rang out their war-steeds' whinny sharp:

And up the sea-salt slopes they wound,
And airs once more of ocean quaff'd:
Those frosty woods the rocks that crown'd
As though May touched them, waved and laugh'd.

And thus they sang, 'Tomorrow morn
Our eyes shall rest upon the foe:
Roll on, swift night, in silence borne,
And blow, thou breeze of sunrise, blow!'

Aubrey de Vere (1814–1902)

from *The Deserted Village*

Beside yon straggling fence that skirts the way,
With blossomed furze unprofitably gay,
There, in his noisy mansion, skilled to rule,
The village master taught his little school:
A man severe he was, and stern to view,
I knew him well, and every truant knew;
Well had the boding tremblers learned to trace
The day's disasters in his morning face;
Full well they laughed with counterfeited glee
At all his jokes, for many a joke had he;
Full well the busy whisper circling round,
Conveyed the dismal tidings when he frowned:
Yet he was kind, or if severe in aught,
The love he bore to learning was in fault;
The village all declared how much he knew,
'Twas certain he could write and cipher too:
Lands he could measure, terms and tides presage,
And e'en the story ran – that he could gauge:
In arguing too, the parson owned his skill,
And e'en though vanquished, he could argue still;
While words of learned length and thund'ring sound,
Amazed the gazing rustics ranged around;
And still they gazed, and still the wonder grew,
That one small head could carry all he knew.
But past is all his fame. The very spot
Where many a time he triumphed, is forgot.

Oliver Goldsmith (1728–74)

Sea-fever

I must down to the seas again, to the lonely sea and the sky,
And all I ask is a tall ship and a star to steer her by,
And the wheel's kick and the wind's song and the white sail's shaking,
And a grey mist on the sea's face and a grey dawn breaking.

I must down to the seas again, for the call of the running tide
Is a wild call and a clear call that may not be denied;
And all I ask is a windy day with the white clouds flying,
And the flung spray and the blown spume, and the sea-gulls crying.

I must down to the seas again, to the vagrant gypsy life,
To the gull's way and the whale's way where the wind's like a whetted knife;
And all I ask is a merry yarn from a laughing fellow-rover,
And quiet sleep and a sweet dream when the long trick's over.

John Masefield (1878–1967)

I Remember, I Remember

I remember, I remember
The house where I was born,
The little window where the sun
Came peeping in at morn;
He never came a wink too soon
Nor brought too long a day;
But now, I often wish the night
Had borne my breath away.

I remember, I remember
The roses, red and white,
The violets, and the lily-cups,
Those flowers made of light!
The lilacs where the robin built,
And where my brother set
The laburnum on his birthday –
The tree is living yet.

I remember, I remember
Where I used to swing,
And thought the air must rush as fresh
To swallows on the wing;
My spirit flew in feathers then
That is so heavy now,
And summer pools could hardly cool
The fever on my brow.

I remember, I remember
The fir trees dark and high;
I used to think their slender tops
Were close against the sky:
It was a childish ignorance,
But now 'tis little joy
To know I'm farther off from Heaven
Than when I was a boy.

Thomas Hood (1799–1845)

A Boy's Song

Where the pools are bright and deep,
Where the grey trout lies asleep,
Up the river and o'er the lea,
That's the way for Billy and me.

Where the blackbird sings the latest,
Where the hawthorn blooms the sweetest,
Where the nestlings chirp and flee,
That's the way for Billy and me.

Where the mowers mow the cleanest,
Where the hay lies thick and greenest –
There to trace the homeward bee,
That's the way for Billy and me.

Where the hazel bank is steepest,
Where the shadow lies the deepest,
Where the clustering nuts fall free,
That's the way for Billy and me.

James Hogg (1770–1835)

The Village Blacksmith

Under the spreading chestnut tree
The village smithy stands;
The smith, a mighty man is he,
With large and sinewy hands;
And the muscles of his brawny arms
Are strong as iron bands.

His hair is crisp, and black, and long;
His face is like the tan;
His brow is wet with honest sweat,
He earns whate'er he can,
And looks the whole world in the face,
For he owes not any man.

Week in, week out, from morn till night,
You can hear his bellows blow;
You can hear him swing his heavy sledge,
With measured beat and slow,
Like a sexton ringing the village bell,
When the evening sun is low.

And children coming home from school
Look in at the open door;
They love to see the flaming forge,
And hear the bellows roar,
And catch the burning sparks that fly
Like chaff from a threshing floor.

He goes on Sunday to the church,
And sits among his boys;
He hears the clergy pray and preach,
He hears his daughter's voice
Singing in the village choir,
And it makes his heart rejoice.

It sounds to him like her mother's voice,
Singing in Paradise!
He needs must think of her once more,
How in the grave she lies;
And with his hard, rough hand he wipes
A tear out of his eyes.

Toiling, – rejoicing, – sorrowing,
Onward through life he goes;
Each morning sees some task begun,
Each evening sees its close;
Something attempted, something done,
Has earned a night's repose.

Thanks, thanks to thee, my worthy friend,
For the lesson thou hast taught!
Thus on the flaming forge of life
Our fortunes must be wrought;
Thus on its sounding anvil shaped
Each burning deed and thought.

Henry Wadsworth Longfellow (1807–82)

Barbara Frietchie

Up from the meadows rich with corn,
Clear in the cool September morn,

The clustered spires of Frederick stand,
Green-walled by the hills of Maryland.

Round about them orchards sweep,
Apple and peach tree fruited deep,

Fair as a garden of the Lord
To the eyes of the famished rebel horde,

On that pleasant morn of the early fall,
When Lee marched over the mountain wall –

Over the mountains winding down,
Horse and foot, into Frederick town.

Forty flags with their silver stars,
Forty flags with their crimson bars,

Flapped in the morning wind: the sun
Of noon looked down and saw not one.

Up rose old Barbara Frietchie then,
Bowed with her fourscore years and ten,

Bravest of all in Frederick town,
She took up the flag the men hauled down;

In her attic window the staff she set,
To show that one heart was loyal yet.

Up the street came the rebel tread,
Stonewall Jackson riding ahead.

Under his slouched hat, left and right,
He glanced: the old flag met his sight.

'Halt!' – the dust-brown ranks stood fast.
'Fire!' – out blazed the rifle-blast.

It shivered the window, pane and sash;
It rent the banner with seam and gash,

Quick, as it fell from the broken staff,
Dame Barbara snatched the silken scarf.

She leaned far out on the window sill,
And shook it forth with a royal will.

'Shoot, if you must, this old grey head,
But spare your country's flag,' she said.

A shade of sadness, a blush of shame,
Over the face of the leader came;

The nobler nature within him stirred
To life at that woman's deed and word.

'Who touches a hair of yon grey head
Dies like a dog! March on!' he said.

All day long through Frederick street
Sounded the tread of marching feet;

All day long the free flag tossed
Over the heads of the rebel host.

Ever its torn folds rose and fell
On the loyal winds that loved it well;

And through the hill-gaps sunset light
Shone over it with a warm good-night.

Barbara Frietchie's work is o'er,
And the rebel rides on his raids no more.

Honour to her! and let a tear
Fall, for her sake, on Stonewall's bier.

Over Barbara Frietchie's grave,
Flag of freedom and union, wave!

Peace and order and beauty draw
Round thy symbol of light and law;

And ever the stars above look down
On thy stars below in Frederick town.

John Greenleaf Whittier (1807–92)

A Psalm of Life

Tell me not, in mournful numbers,
Life is but an empty dream! –
For the soul is dead that slumbers,
And things are not what they seem.

Life is real! Life is earnest!
And the grave is not its goal;
Dust thou art, to dust returnest,
Was not spoken to the soul.

Not enjoyment, and not sorrow,
Is our destined end or way;
But to act, that each tomorrow
Find us farther than today.

Art is long, and Time is fleeting,
And our hearts, though stout and brave,
Still, like muffled drums, are beating
Funeral marches to the grave.

In the world's broad field of battle,
In the bivouac of Life,
Be not like dumb, driven cattle!
Be a hero in the strife!

Trust no Future, howe'er pleasant!
Let the dead Past bury its dead!
Act – act in the living Present!
Heart within, and God o'erhead!

Lives of great men all remind us
We can make our lives sublime,
And, departing, leave behind us,
Footprints on the sand of time;

Footprints, that perhaps another,
Sailing o'er life's solemn main,
A forlorn and shipwrecked brother,
Seeing, shall take heart again.

Let us, then, be up and doing,
With a heart for any fate;
Still achieving, still pursuing,
Learn to labour and to wait.

Henry Wadsworth Longfellow (1807–82)

My Shadow

I have a little shadow that goes in and out with me
And what can be the use of him is more than I can see;
He is very, very like me from heel up to the head,
And I see him jump before me, when I jump into my bed.

The funniest thing about him is the way he likes to grow –
Not at all like proper children, which is always very slow;
For he sometimes shoots up taller like an India-rubber ball,
And he sometimes gets so little that there is none of him at all.

He hasn't got a notion of how children ought to play,
And can only make a fool of me in every kind of way;
He stays so close beside me, he's a coward you can see;
I'd think shame to stick to Nursie as that shadow sticks to me.

One morning very early, before the sun was up,
I rose and found the shining dew on every buttercup;
But my lazy little shadow, like an errant sleepy-head,
Had stayed at home behind me, and was fast asleep in bed.

Robert Louis Stevenson (1850–94)

Leisure

What is this life if, full of care,
We have no time to stand and stare.

No time to stand beneath the boughs
And stare as long as sheep or cows.

No time to see, when woods we pass,
Where squirrels hide their nuts in grass.

No time to see, in broad daylight,
Streams full of stars, like skies at night.

No time to turn at Beauty's glance,
And watch her feet, how they can dance.

A poor life this if, full of care,
We have no time to stand and stare.

William H. Davies (1871–1940)

The Daffodils

I wandered lonely as a cloud
That floats on high o'er vales and hills,
When all at once I saw a crowd,
A host of golden daffodils;
Beside the lake, beneath the trees,
Fluttering and dancing in the breeze.

Continuous as the stars that shine
And twinkle on the Milky Way,
They stretch'd in never-ending line
Along the margin of a bay;
Ten thousand saw I at a glance
Tossing their heads in sprightly dance.

The waves beside them danced, but they
Out-did the sparkling waves in glee.
A poet could not but be gay
In such a jocund company!
I gazed – and gazed – but little thought
What wealth the show to me had brought:

For oft, when on my couch I lie
In vacant or in pensive mood,
They flash upon that inward eye
Which is the bliss of solitude;
And then my heart with pleasure fills,
And dances with the daffodils.

William Wordsworth (1770–1850)

Signs of Rain

The hollow winds begin to blow,
The clouds look black, the glass is low.

The soot falls down, the spaniels sleep,
The spiders from their cobwebs peep.

Last night the sun went pale to bed,
The moon in haloes hid her head.

The boding shepherd heaves a sigh,
For, see, a rainbow in the sky.

The walls are damp, the ditches smell,
Closed is the pink-eyed pimpernel.

Hark how the chairs and tables crack!
Old Betty's joints are on the rack.

Loud quack the ducks, the peacocks cry,
The distant hills are seeming nigh.

How restless are the snorting swine;
The busy flies disturb the kine.

Low o'er the grass the swallow wings,
The cricket, too, how sharp he sings.

Puss on the hearth with velvet paws,
Sits wiping o'er her whiskered jaws.

Through the clear stream the fishes rise,
And nimbly catch the incautious flies.

The glow-worms, numerous and bright,
Illumed the dewy dell last night.

At dusk the squalid toad was seen,
Hopping and crawling o'er the green.

The whirling wind the dust obeys,
And in the rapid eddy plays.

The frog has changed his yellow vest,
And in a russet coat is dressed.

Though June, the air is cold and still,
The mellow blackbird's voice is shrill.

My dog, so altered in his taste,
Quits mutton-bones on grass to feast.

And see yon rooks, how odd their flight,
They imitate the gliding kite;

And seem precipitate to fall,
As if they felt the piercing ball.

'Twill surely rain, I see with sorrow,
Our jaunt must be put off tomorrow.

Edward Jenner (1749–1823)

The Brook

I come from haunts of coot and hern,
I make a sudden sally
And sparkle out among the fern,
To bicker down a valley.

By thirty hills I hurry down,
Or slip between the ridges,
By twenty thorps, a little town,
And half a hundred bridges.

Till last by Philip's farm I flow
To join the brimming river,
For men may come and men may go,
But I go on for ever.

I chatter over stony ways,
In little sharps and trebles,
I bubble into eddying bays,
I babble on the pebbles.

With many a curve my banks I fret
By many a field and fallow,
And many a fairy foreland set
With willow-weed and mallow.

I chatter, chatter, as I flow
To join the brimming river,
For men may come and men may go,
But I go on for ever.

I wind about, and in and out,
With here a blossom sailing,
And here and there a lusty trout,
And here and there a grayling,

And here and there a foamy flake
Upon me, as I travel,
With many a silvery waterbreak
Above the golden gravel,

And draw them all along, and flow
To join the brimming river,
For men may come and men may go,
But I go on for ever.

I steal by lawns and grassy plots,
I slide by hazel covers;
I move the sweet forget-me-nots
That grow for happy lovers.

I slip, I slide, I gloom, I glance,
Among my skimming swallows;
I make the nettled sunbeam dance
Against my sandy shallows.

I murmur under moon and stars
In brambly wildernesses;
I linger by my shingly bars;
I loiter round my cresses;

And out again I curve and flow,
To join the brimming river,
For men may come and men may go,
But I go on for ever.

Alfred Lord Tennyson (1809–92)

Lord Ullin's Daughter

A Chieftain to the Highlands bound
Cries, 'Boatman, do not tarry!
And I'll give thee a silver pound
To row us o'er the ferry!'

'Now who be ye, would cross Lochgyle,
This dark and stormy water?'
'O I'm the chief of Ulva's isle,
And this, Lord Ullin's daughter.

'And fast before her father's men
Three days we've fled together,
For should he find us in the glen,
My blood would stain the heather.

'His horsemen hard behind us ride –
Should they our steps discover,
Then who will cheer my bonny bride,
When they have slain her lover?'

Out spoke the hardy Highland wight,
'I'll go, my chief, I'm ready:
It is not for your silver bright,
But for your winsome lady: –

'And by my word! the bonny bird
In danger shall not tarry;
So though the waves are raging white
I'll row you o'er the ferry.'

By this the storm grew loud apace,
The water-wraith was shrieking;
And in the scowl of Heaven each face
Grew dark as they were speaking.

But still as wilder blew the wind,
And as the night grew drearer,
Adown the glen rode armèd men,
Their trampling sounded nearer.

'O haste thee, haste!' the lady cries,
'Though tempests round us gather;
I'll meet the raging of the skies,
But not an angry father.'

The boat has left a stormy land,
A stormy sea before her, –
When, oh! too strong for human hand
The tempest gather'd o'er her.

And still they row'd amidst the roar
Of waters fast prevailing:
Lord Ullin reach'd that fatal shore, –
His wrath was changed to wailing.

For, sore dismay'd, through storm and shade
His child he did discover: –
One lovely hand she stretch'd for aid,
And one was round her lover.

'Come back! come back!' he cried in grief,
'Across this stormy water:
And I'll forgive your Highland chief,
My daughter! – Oh, my daughter!'

'Twas vain: the loud waves lash'd the shore,
Return or aid preventing:
The waters wild went o'er his child,
And he was left lamenting.

Thomas Campbell (1777–1844)

Lucy Gray

Oft I had heard of Lucy Gray:
And, when I cross'd the wild,
I chanced to see at break of day
The solitary child.

No mate, no comrade Lucy knew;
She dwelt on a wide moor,
The sweetest thing that ever grew
Beside a human door!

You yet may spy the fawn at play,
The hare upon the green;
But the sweet face of Lucy Gray
Will never more be seen.

'Tonight will be a stormy night –
You to the town must go;
And take a lantern, Child, to light
Your mother through the snow.'

'That, father! will I gladly do:
'Tis scarcely afternoon –
The minster-clock has just struck two,
And yonder is the moon!'

At this the father raised his hook,
And snapp'd a faggot-band;
He plied his work; – and Lucy took
The lantern in her hand.

Not blither is the mountain roe:
With many a wanton stroke
Her feet disperse the powdery snow,
That rises up like smoke.

The storm came on before its time;
She wander'd up and down;
And many a hill did Lucy climb:
But never reach'd the town.

The wretched parents all that night
Went shouting far and wide;
But there was neither sound nor sight
To serve them for a guide.

At day-break on a hill they stood
That overlook'd the moor;
And thence they saw the bridge of wood
A furlong from their door.

They wept – and, turning homeward, cried
'In heaven we all shall meet!'
– When in the snow the mother spied
The print of Lucy's feet.

Then downwards from the steep hill's edge
They track'd the footmarks small;
And through the broken hawthorn hedge,
And by the long stone-wall:

And then an open field they cross'd:
The marks were still the same;
They tracked them on, nor ever lost;
And to the bridge they came:

They follow'd from the snowy bank
Those footmarks, one by one,
Into the middle of the plank;
And further there were none!

– Yet some maintain that to this day
She is a living child;
That you may see sweet Lucy Gray
Upon the lonesome wild.

O'er rough and smooth she trips along
And never looks behind;
And sings a solitary song
That whistles in the wind.

William Wordsworth (1770–1850)

Casabianca

The boy stood on the burning deck, whence all, but he, had fled;
The flames, that lit the battle's wreck, shone round him o'er the dead.
Yet beautiful and bright he stood, as born to rule the storm;
A creature of heroic blood, a proud, though childlike form!

The flames rolled on – he would not go without his father's word;
That father, faint in death below, his voice no longer heard.
He called aloud: 'Say, father, say, if yet my task is done?'
He knew not that the chieftain lay, unconscious of his son.

'Speak, father!' once again he cried, 'if I may yet be gone?'
But now the booming shots replied, and fast the flames rolled on:
Upon his brow he felt their breath, and in his waving hair,
And looked from that lone post of death, in still, yet brave despair,

And shouted but once more, aloud: 'My father, must I stay?'
While o'er him fast, through sail and shroud, the wreathing fires made way.
They wrapt the ship in splendour wild, they caught the flag on high,
They streamed above the gallant child, like banners in the sky.

There came a burst of thunder-sound; – the boy – Oh! where was he?
Ask of the winds that far around with fragments strewed the sea,
With mast and helm and pennon fair, that well had borne their part:
But the noblest thing that perished there, was that young faithful heart.

Felicia Hemans (1794–1835)

Lochinvar

O young Lochinvar is come out of the west,
Through all the wide Border his steed was the best;
And save his good broadsword he weapons had none,
He rode all unarm'd, and he rode all alone.
So faithful in love, and so dauntless in war,
There never was knight like the young Lochinvar.

He staid not for brake, and he stopp'd not for stone,
He swam the Eske river where ford there was none;
But ere he alighted at Netherby gate,
The bride had consented, the gallant came late:
For a laggard in love, and a dastard in war,
Was to wed the fair Ellen of brave Lochinvar.

So boldly he enter'd the Netherby hall,
Among bride's-men, and kinsmen, and brothers, and all:
Then spoke the bride's father, his hand on his sword,
(For the poor craven bridegroom said never a word),
'O come ye in peace here, or come ye in war,
Or to dance at our bridal, young Lord Lochinvar?'

'I long woo'd your daughter, my suit you denied; –
Love swells like the Solway, but ebbs like its tide –
And now am I come, with this lost love of mine,
To lead but one measure, drink one cup of wine.
There are maidens in Scotland more lovely by far,
That would gladly be bride to the young Lochinvar.'

The bride kiss'd the goblet: the knight took it up,
He quaff'd off the wine, and he threw down the cup.
She look'd down to blush, and she look'd up to sigh,
With a smile on her lips, and a tear in her eye.
He took her soft hand, ere her mother could bar,
'Now tread we a measure!' said young Lochinvar.

So stately his form, and so lovely her face,
That never a hall such a galliard did grace;
While her mother did fret, and her father did fume,
And the bridegroom stood dangling his bonnet and plume;
And the bride-maidens whisper'd, "Twere better by far,
To have match'd our fair cousin with young Lochinvar.'

One touch to her hand, and one word in her ear,
When they reach'd the hall-door, and the charger stood near;
So light to the croupe the fair lady he swung,
So light to the saddle before her he sprung!
'She is won! we are gone, over bank, bush, and scaur;
They'll have fleet steeds that follow,' quoth young Lochinvar.

There was mounting 'mong Graemes of the Netherby clan;
Forsters, Fenwicks, and Musgraves, they rode and they ran:
There was racing and chasing, on Cannobie Lee,
But the lost bride of Netherby ne'er did they see.
So daring in love, and so dauntless in war,
Have ye e'er heard of gallant like young Lochinvar?

Sir Walter Scott (1771–1832)

She is Far from the Land

She is far from the land where her young hero sleeps,
And lovers are round her sighing;
But coldly she turns from their gaze and weeps,
For her heart is in his grave lying.

She sings the wild song of her dear native plains,
Every note which he loved awaking; –
Ah! little they think, who delight in their strains,
How the heart of the Minstrel is breaking.

He had lived for his love, for his country he died,
They were all that to life had entwined him;
Nor soon shall the tears of his country be dried,
Nor long will his love stay behind him.

Oh! make her a grave where the sunbeams rest
When they promise a glorious morrow;
They'll shine o'er her sleep, like a smile from the west,
From her own loved island of sorrow.

Thomas Moore (1799–1852)

The Wreck of the Hesperus

It was the schooner Hesperus,
That sailed the wintry sea;
And the skipper had taken his little daughter,
To bear him company.

Blue were her eyes as the fairy-flax,
Her cheeks like the dawn of day,
And her bosom white as the hawthorn buds
That ope in the month of May.

The skipper he stood beside the helm,
His pipe was in his mouth,
And he watched how the veering flaw did blow
The smoke now West, now South.

Then up and spake an old Sailor,
Had sailed the Spanish Main,
'I pray thee, put into yonder port,
For I fear a hurricane.

'Last night the moon had a golden ring,
And tonight no moon we see!'
The skipper he blew a whiff from his pipe,
And a scornful laugh laughed he.

Colder and colder blew the wind,
A gale from the North-east,
The snow fell hissing in the brine,
And the billows frothed like yeast.

Down came the storm, and smote amain
The vessel in its strength;
She shuddered and paused, like a frightened steed,
Then leaped her cable's length.

'Come hither! come hither! my little daughter,
And do not tremble so;
For I can weather the roughest gale
That ever wind did blow.'

He wrapped her warm in his seaman's coat
Against the stinging blast;
He cut a rope from a broken spar,
And bound her to the mast.

'O father! I hear the church-bell ring,
O say, what may it be?'
'Tis a fog-bell on a rock-bound coast!' –
And he steered for the open sea.

'O father! I hear the sound of guns,
O say, what may it be?'
'Some ship in distress, that cannot live .
In such an angry sea!'

'O father! I see a gleaming light,
O say, what may it be?'
But the father answered never a word,
A frozen corpse was he.

Lashed to the helm, all stiff and stark,
With his face turned to the skies,
The lantern gleamed through the gleaming snow
On his fixed and glassy eyes.

Then the maiden clasped her hands and prayed
That saved she might be;
And she thought of Christ, who stilled the wave
On the lake of Galilee.

And fast through the midnight dark and drear,
Through the whistling sleet and snow,
Like a sheeted ghost the vessel swept
Towards the reef of Norman's Woe.

And ever the fitful gusts between
A sound came from the land;
It was the sound of the trampling surf
On the rocks and the hard sea-sand.

The breakers were right beneath her bows,
She drifted a dreary wreck,
And a whooping billow swept the crew
Like icicles from her deck.

She struck where the white and fleecy waves
Looked soft as carded wool,
But the cruel rocks they gored her side
Like the horns of an angry bull.

Her rattling shrouds, all sheathed in ice,
With the masts went by the board;
Like a vessel of glass she stove and sank,
Ho! ho! the breakers roared!

At daybreak on the bleak sea-beach
A fisherman stood aghast,
To see the form of a maiden fair
Lashed close to a drifting mast.

The salt sea was frozen on her breast,
The salt tears in her eyes;
And he saw her hair, like the brown sea-weed,
On the billows fall and rise.

Such was the wreck of the Hesperus,
In the midnight and the snow!
Christ save us all from a death like this,
On the reef of Norman's Woe!

Henry Wadsworth Longfellow (1807–82)

The Listeners

'Is there anybody there?' said the Traveller,
Knocking on the moonlit door;
And his horse in the silence champed the grasses
Of the forest's ferny floor:
And a bird flew up out of the turret,
Above the Traveller's head:
And he smote upon the door again a second time;
'Is there anybody there?' he said.
But no one descended to the Traveller;
No head from the leaf-fringed sill
Leaned over and looked into his grey eyes,
Where he stood perplexed and still.
But only a host of phantom listeners
That dwelt in that lone house then
Stood listening in the quiet of the moonlight
To that voice from the world of men:
Stood thronging the faint moonbeams on the dark stair,
That goes down to the empty hall,
Hearkening in an air stirred and shaken
By the lonely Traveller's call.
And he felt in his heart their strangeness,
Their stillness answering his cry,
While his horse moved, cropping the dark turf,
'Neath the starred and leafy sky;
For he suddenly smote on the door, even
Louder, and lifted his head: –
'Tell them I came,' and no one answered,
That I kept my word,' he said.

Never the least stir made the listeners,
Though every word he spake
Fell echoing through the shadowiness of the still house
From the one man left awake:
Ay, they heard his foot upon the stirrup,
And the sound of iron on stone,
And how the silence surged softly backward,
When the plunging hoofs were gone.

Walter de la Mare (1873–1956)

Little Boy Blue

The little toy dog is covered with dust,
But sturdy and staunch he stands;
The little toy soldier is red with rust,
And his musket moulds in his hands.
Time was when the little toy dog was new,
And the soldier was passing fair;
And that was the time when our Little Boy Blue
Kissed them and put them there.

'Now don't you go till I come,' he said,
'And don't you make any noise!'
Then, toddling off to his trundle-bed,
He dreamt of his pretty toys;
And, as he was dreaming, an angel song
Awakened our Little Boy Blue –
Oh! the years are many, the years are long,
But the little toy friends are true.

Aye, faithful to Little Boy Blue they stand,
Each in the same old place –
Awaiting the touch of a little hand,
The smile of a little face;
And they wonder, waiting the long years through,
In the dust of that little chair,
What has become of our Little Boy Blue,
Since he kissed them and put them there.

Eugene Field (1850–95)

Break, Break, Break

Break, break, break,
On thy cold grey stones, O Sea!
And I would that my tongue could utter
The thoughts that arise in me.

O well for the fisherman's boy,
That he shouts with his sister at play!
O well for the sailor lad,
That he sings in his boat on the bay!

And the stately ships go on
To their haven under the hill;
But O for the touch of a vanish'd hand,
And the sound of a voice that is still!

Break, break, break,
At the foot of thy crags, O Sea!
But the tender grace of a day that is dead
Will never come back to me.

Alfred Lord Tennyson (1809–92)

Young and Old

When all the world is young, lad,
And all the trees are green;
And every goose a swan, lad,
And every lass a queen;
Then hey for boot and horse, lad,
And round the world away;
Young blood must have its course, lad,
And every dog his day.

When all the world is old, lad,
And all the trees are brown;
And all the sport is stale, lad,
And all the wheels run down;
Creep home, and take your place there,
The spent and maimed among;
God grant you find one face there,
You loved when all was young.

Charles Kingsley (1819–75)

from *Elegy Written in a Country Churchyard*

The curfew tolls the knell of parting day,
The lowing herd wind slowly o'er the lea,
The ploughman homeward plods his weary way,
And leaves the world to darkness and to me.

. . .

Beneath those rugged elms, that yew-tree's shade,
Where heaves the turf in many a mouldering heap,
Each in his narrow cell for ever laid,
The rude forefathers of the hamlet sleep.

. . .

For them no more the blazing hearth shall burn,
Or busy housewife ply her evening care;
No children run to lisp their sire's return,
Or climb his knees the envied kiss to share.

Oft did the harvest to their sickle yield,
Their furrow oft the stubborn glebe has broke;
How jocund did they drive their team afield!
How bowed the woods beneath their sturdy stroke!

Let not Ambition mock their useful toil,
Their homely joys, and destiny obscure;
Nor Grandeur hear with a disdainful smile
The short and simple annals of the poor.

The boast of heraldry, the pomp of power,
And all that beauty, all that wealth e'er gave,
Awaits alike th' inevitable hour: –
The paths of glory lead but to the grave.

. . .

Perhaps in this neglected spot is laid
Some heart once pregnant with celestial fire;
Hands that the rod of empire might have swayed,
Or waked to ecstasy the living lyre:

But knowledge to their eyes her ample page
Rich with the spoils of time did ne'er unroll:
Chill Penury repressed their noble rage,
And froze the genial current of the soul.

Full many a gem of purest ray serene
The dark unfathomed caves of ocean bear;
Full many a flower is born to blush unseen,
And waste its sweetness on the desert air.

. . .

Far from the madding crowd's ignoble strife
Their sober wishes never learned to stray;
Along the cool sequestered vale of life
They kept the noiseless tenor of their way . . .

Thomas Gray (1716–71)

Requiem

Under the wide and starry sky,
Dig the grave and let me lie.
Glad did I live and gladly die,
And I laid me down with a will.

This be the verse you grave for me:
Here he lies where he longed to be;
Home is the sailor, home from sea,
And the hunter home from the hill.

Robert Louis Stevenson (1850–94)

Crossing the Bar

Sunset and evening star,
And one clear call for me!
And may there be no moaning of the bar,
When I put out to sea.

But such a tide as moving seems asleep,
Too full for sound and foam,
When that which drew from out the boundless deep
Turns again home.

Twilight and evening bell,
And after that the dark!
And may there be no sadness of farewell,
When I embark;

For tho' from out our bourne of Time and Place
The flood may bear me far,
I hope to see my Pilot face to face
When I have crost the bar.

Alfred Lord Tennyson (1809–92)

An Gleann 'Nar Tógadh Mé

Ó ait go háit ba bhreá mo shiúl
'S dob ard mo léim ar bharr an tsléibh',
San uisce fíor ba mhór mo dhúil,
'S ba bheo mo chroí i lár mo chléibh;
Mar chos an ghiorria do bhí mo chos,
Mar iarann gach alt is féith,
Bhí an sonas romham, thall 's abhus,
Sa ghleann 'nar tógadh mé.

Ba chuma liomsa fear ar bith,
Ba chuma liom an domhan iomlán,
Mar rith an fhia do bhí mo rith,
Mar shruth an tsléibh' ag dul le fán;
Is ní raibh rud ar bith sa domhan
Nach ndéanfainn (dá mba mhaith liom é);
Do léim mo bhád ar bharr na habhann
Sa ghleann 'nar tógadh mé.

Gach ní dá bhfacas le mo shúil
Bhí sé, dar liom, ar dhath an óir;
Is annamh a dhearcainn ar mo chúl
Ach ag dul ar aghaidh le misneach mór;
Do leanainnse gan stad gan scíth
Mo rún, nuair chuirinn romham é;
Do bhéarfainn, dar liom, ar an ngaoth
Sa ghleann 'nar tógadh mé.

Ní hamhlaidh tá sé liom anois!
Do bhí mé luath, 'nois tá mé mall;
Is é mo léan, an aois do bhris
Sean-neart mo chroí is lúth mo bhall;
Do chaill mé mórán 's fuair mé fios
Ar mhórán − och! ní sású é −
Mo léan! mo léan! gan mé aris óg
Sa ghleann 'nar tógadh mé.

Dúghlás de Híde (1860–1949)

— 94 —

SPINNING WOOL FOR "DONEGAL HOMESPUN", INISHOWEN.   WAG 1181.

Bean tSléibhe ag Caoineadh a Mic

Brón ar an mbás, 'sé dhubh mo chroíse,
D'fhuadaigh mo ghrá is d'fhág mé cloíte
Gan charaid gan chompánach faoi dhíon mo thíse,
Ach an léan seo im' lár, is mé ag caoineadh!

Ag gabháil an tsléibhe dhom tráthnóna
Do labhair an éanlaith liom go brónach,
Do labhair an naosc binn 's an crotach glórach
Ag faisnéis dom gur éag mo stórach.

Do ghlaoigh mé ort is do ghlór níor chualas,
Do ghlaoigh mé arís is freagra ní bhfuaireas,
Do phóg mé do bhéal, is a Dhia, nárbh fhuar é! -
Och, is fuar í do leaba sa chillín uaigneach.

'S a uaigh fhódghlas ina bhfuil mo leanbh,
A uaigh chaol bheag, ós tú a leaba,
Mo bheannacht ort, 's na mílte beannacht
Ar na fóda glasa atá os cionn mo pheata.

Brón ar an mbás, ní féidir a shéanadh,
Leagann sé úr is críon le chéile -
'S a mhaicín mhánla, is é mo chéasadh
Do cholainn chaomh bheith ag déanamh créafóig'.

Pádraig Mac Piarais (1879–1916)

Tháinig Long ó Valparaiso

Tháinig long ó Valparaiso,
Scaoileadh téad a seol sa chuan;
Chuir a hainm dom i gcuimhne
Ríocht na gréine, tír na mbua.

'Gluais,' ar sí, 'ar thuras fada
Liom ó scamall is ó cheo;
Tá fé shleasaibh gorm-Andes
Cathair scáfar, glé mar sheod.'

Ach bhíos óg is ní imeoinnse,
Am an dóchais, tús mo shaoil;
Chreideas fós go raibh i ndán dom
Iontaisí na ndán 's na scéal.

Ghluais an long thar linntibh mara
Fad' ó shin 's a crann mar ór,
Scríobh a scéal ar phár na hoíche,
Ard i rian na réiltean mór.

Fillfidh sí arís chugam, áfach;
Chífead cathair bhán fén sléibh
Le hais Mara na Síochána -
Creidim fós beagnach, a Dhé.

Pádraig de Brún (1889–1960)

Anseo i Lár an Ghleanna

Bhí an tAifreann léite is gach rud déanta,
Bhí pobal Dé ag scaipeadh
Nuair chualamar gleo ag teacht 'nár dtreo
Anseo i lár an ghleanna.

'Cén gleo é siúd ag teacht 'nár dtreo?'
'Sin torann cos na gcapall.'
'Seo chugainn saighdiúirí arm an rí
Anseo i lár an ghleanna.'

Do chas an seanfhear Brian Ó Laoi
Is shiúil i dtreo an tsagairt,
Is chuir sé cogar ina chluais
Anseo i lár an ghleanna.

'Ó a Athair Seán, Ó a Athair Séan,
Seo chugainn na cótaí dearga;
Ní féidir leatsa teitheadh anois
Anseo i lár an ghleanna.

'Tá tusa óg, a Athair Seán,
Táim féin i ndeireadh beatha;
Déan malairt éadaigh liom anois
Anseo i lár an ghleanna.'

Do deineadh malairt gan rómhoill
I gcoinne thoil an tsagairt,
Is shíl sé deora móra bróin
Anseo i lár an ghleanna.

Do ghabh na Sasanaigh Brian Ó Laoi,
Is d'imigh saor an sagart;
Do chroch siad Brian ar chrann caol ard
Anseo i lár an ghleanna.

Ach mairfidh cáil an tseanfhir áigh
Faid fhásfaidh féar ar thalamh;
Beidh a scéal á ríomh ag fearaibh Fáil,
Is anseo i lár an ghleanna.

Seán Mac Fheorais (1915–84)

Cúl an Tí

Tá Tír na nÓg ar chúl an tí,
Tír álainn trína chéile,
Lucht ceithre chos ag siúl na slí
Gan bróga orthu ná léine,
Gan Béarla acu ná Gaeilge.

Ach fásann clóca ar gach droim
Sa tír seo trína chéile,
Is labhartar teanga ar chúl an tí
Nár thuig aon fhear ach Aesop,
Is tá sé siúd sa chré anois.

Tá cearca ann is ál sicín,
Is lacha righin mhothaolach,
Is gadhar mór dubh mar namhaid sa tír
Ag drannadh le gach éinne,
Is cat ag crú na gréine.

Sa chúinne thiar tá banc dramhaíl'
Is iontaisí an tsaoil ann,
Coinnleoir, búclaí, seanhata tuí,
Is trúmpa balbh néata,
Is citeal bán mar ghé ann.

Is ann a thagann tincéirí
Go naofa, trína chéile,
Tá gaol acu le cúl an tí
Is bíd ag iarraidh déirce
Ar chúl gach tí in Éirinn.

Ba mhaith liom bheith ar chúl an tí
Sa doircheacht go déanach,
Go bhfeicfinn ann ar chuairt gealaí
An t-ollaimhín sin Aesop
Is é ina phúca léannta.

Seán Ó Ríordáin (1917–1977)

PLAYING "WEE SHOP"   WAG 338

A Dhroimeann Donn Dílis

A dhroimeann donn dílis, a shíoda na mbó,
Cá ngabhann tú san oíche 's cá mbíonn tú sa ló?
Bímse ar na coillte 's mo bhuachaill im' chomhair,
'S d'fhág sé siúd mise ag sileadh na ndeor.

Níl fearann, níl tíos agam, níl fíonta ná ceol,
Níl flatha im choimhdeacht, níl saoithe ná sló;
Ach ag síor-ól an uisce go minic sa ló,
Agus beathuisce 's fíon ag mo naimhde ar bord.

Dá bhfaighinnse cead aighnis nó radharc ar an gcoróin,
Sasanaigh do leadhbfainn mar do leadhbfainn seanbhróg,
Trí bhogaigh, trí choillte 's trí dhraighneach lá ceo,
Is siúd mar a bhréagfainnse an droimeann donn Ó.

Ón mbéaloideas

Labhair an Teanga Ghaeilge

Ó labhair an teanga Ghaeilge liom,
A chuid mo chroí is a stór,
An teanga a labhair mo mháthair liom,
In Éirinn ghlas fadó.
'Sí teanga bhinn ár sinsear í,
An chaint is milse glór:
Ó labhair an teanga Ghaeilge liom,
Is bain dem' chroí an brón.

Ó labhair an teanga Ghaeilge liom,
'Sí teanga cheart na nGael:
An teanga bhinn is ársa 'tá
Lé fáil ar fud an tsaoil.
A stór mo chroí is beannacht ort,
A chailin óig gan cháim,
Cá bhfuil sa saol aon teanga mar
Ár dteanga féin le fáil?

Ní fios cé a chum

Cill Aodáin

Anois teacht an earraigh beidh an lá 'dul 'un síneadh,
'S tar éis na Féil' Bríde ardóidh mé mo sheol;
Ó chuir mé 'mo cheann é ní chónóidh mé choíche
Go seasfaidh mé síos i lár Chontae Mhaigh Eo.
I gClár Chlainne Mhuiris a bheas mé an chéad oíche,
'S i mBalla taobh thíos de thosós mé ag ól;
Go Coillte Mach rachad go ndéanad cuairt mhíosa ann,
I bhfogas dhá mhíle do Bhéal an Áth' Móir.

Fágaim le huacht é go n-éiríonn mo chroíse,
Mar éiríos an ghaoth nó mar scaipeas an ceo,
Nuair smaoiním ar Cheara nó ar Ghaileang taobh thíos de,
Ar Sceathach a' Mhíle 's ar phlánaí Mhaigh Eo;
Cill Aodáin an baile a bhfásann gach ní ann –
Tá sméara 's sú craobh ann is meas ar gach sórt;
'S dá mbeinnse 'mo sheasamh i gceartlár mo dhaoine,
D'imeodh an aois díom is bheinn arís óg.

Antaine Ó Reachtaire (1784–1835)

Biographical Notes

Cecil Frances Alexander (1818–95) was born in County Wicklow. In 1850 she married a clergyman, William Alexander, who became Bishop of Derry and later Primate of Ireland. There are very few people who have not heard of her most famous works: 'All Things Bright and Beautiful', 'Once in Royal David's City' and 'There is a Green Hill Far Away'.

William Allingham (1824–89) was born in Ballyshannon, County Donegal, and at the age of fourteen became a clerk in the local bank, of which his father was manager. He later served as a customs officer in the north of Ireland before being transferred to England. Most of his poems, such as 'Adieu to Ballashanney', are about his native Donegal.

Mary Dow Brine (*fl.* 1878) is a poet about almost nothing is known, though her poem 'A Noble Boy' was well known to a generation of Irish schoolchildren

Joseph Campbell (1879–1944) was born in Belfast and educated at St Malachy's College. He became a leading figure of the Ulster Literary Theatre and his play, *Judgment*, was produced at the Abbey Theatre in 1913. In 1925 he went to New York, where he spent fifteen years at Fordham University and founded the School of Irish Studies. He returned to Ireland and spent his latter years in County Wicklow.

Thomas Campbell (1777–1844) was the son of a Glasgow merchant. He is best remembered for his splendid war songs, 'Hohenlinden', 'The Battle of the Baltic' and 'Ye Mariners of England', as well as for his dramatic poems, 'Lord Ullin's Daughter' and 'Lochiel's Warning'. Campbell was also a great reformer and one of the founders of London University.

Padraic Colum (1881–1972) was born in County Longford and wrote plays and novels as well as poetry. He was an associate of Yeats, Synge, Æ and Lady Gregory and was one of the first playwrights of the Abbey Theatre. In 1914 he went to America and he spent much of his life in New York. His lyrics of Irish rural life, especially 'The Old Woman of the Roads', 'The Drover' and the famous ballad 'She Moved through the Fair', have been included in many anthologies of English verse. He is buried in Sutton, County Dublin.

William H. Davies (1871–1940) was born in poverty in Newport in Wales. He spent much of his life as a pedlar on the streets. He went to America at the age of twenty-two and had his right leg severed at the ankle while trying to jump a freight train. His first book of verse appeared in England in 1905. Bernard Shaw helped to establish his reputation. His most famous work is *The Autobiography of a Super-Tramp*.

Monsignor Pádraig de Brún (1889–1960) was born in County Tipperary and was ordained to the priesthood at Clonliffe College in 1913. He attended University College Dublin and was a professor in Maynooth College for many years. In 1945 he was appointed President of University College Galway. He had a great knowledge of languages, and translated many literary works into Irish.

Dúghlás de Híde (1860–1949) was born in County Roscommon. He founded the Gaelic League in 1893 and became Professor of Modern Irish at the National University. He was a prolific writer and translator and was the driving force of the Irish Literary Revival. In 1938 he became the first President of Ireland.

Walter de la Mare (1873–1956) was born in Kent and educated at St Paul's School in London. He spent eighteen years as a clerk before taking up writing as a full-time profession. He published a large body of poetry and children's verse. He was fascinated by the supernatural and loved ghost stories and tales of fantasy.

Aubrey de Vere (1814–1902) was born in Adare, County Limerick, and educated at Trinity College Dublin. He published several volumes of verse, including *Innisfail*, a series of poems about the chief events in certain epochs of Irish history.

Eugene Field (1850–95) was an American poet who wrote poems for children, the most famous of which are 'A Dutch Lullaby' and 'Little Boy Blue'.

Oliver Goldsmith (1728–74), poet, playwright, novelist and essay writer, was born in County Longford. He studied medicine but did not practise. Instead he turned to writing, went to London and became an associate of Samuel Johnson, Edmund Burke and Joshua Reynolds. His most famous works are the novel *The Vicar of Wakefield*, the play *She Stoops to Conquer*, and the poem 'The Deserted Village'.

Thomas Gray (1716–71) was born in London and educated at Eton and Cambridge, where he became Professor of History. Unlike many of his contemporaries, Gray preferred to write about nature, and his verse, like Goldsmith's, appealed to the emotions as well as to the intellect.

Gerald Griffin (1803–40) was born in Limerick. He went to London at an early age with hopes of becoming a successful dramatist, but although he wrote a certain amount of verse and a relatively well-received novel, *The Collegians*, he became disillusioned and burnt all his manuscripts. He joined the Christian Brothers order and died two years later.

Felicia Hemans (1794–1835) was born in Liverpool, the daughter of an Irishman who had settled as a merchant there. She came to live in Dublin in her later years and is buried in a vault beneath St Ann's Church, Dawson Street.

James Hogg (1770–1835) was born in Ettrick Forest and became a shepherd. His poetry was discovered by Sir Walter Scott. He went to Edinburgh in 1810 and became acquainted with Byron, Wordsworth and Southey. He was a contributor to *Blackwood's Magazine* and is best remembered for his poetical work 'The Queen's Wake'.

Thomas Hood (1799–1845), the son of a bookseller, is best remembered for his humorous work, but he also wrote a number of serious poems, such as 'The Bridge of Sighs', 'Time of Roses' and 'The Death-Bed'. He was an associate of Lamb, Hazlitt and De Quincey.

Dr Edward Jenner (1749–1823) was a British physician who developed the first effective vaccine against smallpox. His findings led to the widespread use of vaccination as a protective measure.

John Keats (1795–1821) was born in London and originally trained as a doctor. He was one of the most celebrated of the Romantic poets, famous especially for his odes, such as 'Ode to a Nightingale' and 'Ode on a Grecian Urn'. He died of tuberculosis in Rome at the age of twenty-six.

Joyce Kilmer (1886–1918) was born in New Brunswick, New Jersey, and educated at Columbia University. He claimed to be 'half Irish' and joined an Irish regiment, the 'Fighting Sixty-Ninth', to fight in the Great War in France. He was killed near Ourq in 1918.

Charles Kingsley (1819–75) was born in Devonshire. He was a Victorian polymath, a clergyman, naturalist, historian, poet and polemicist. He is best remembered as the author of *Westward Ho!* and *The Water Babies*.

Francis Ledwidge (1891–1917) was born in Slane, County Meath, where his childhood was spent in poverty. He worked as a labourer and a grocer's apprentice. Lord Dunsany recognised his talents as a poet and helped him with the publication of his books of verse. Ledwidge joined Redmond's National Volunteers and later enlisted in the Inniskilling Fusiliers. He was killed in action in France in the First World War.

Henry Wadsworth Longfellow (1807–82) was educated at Harvard and became Professor of Modern Languages there in 1836, having first travelled extensively in Europe. He visited London in 1842 and was the guest of Charles Dickens. His best-known works are 'The Psalm of Life', 'The Wreck of the Hesperus' and 'Hiawatha'.

Seán Mac Fheorais (1915–84) was born in County Kildare and educated through Irish. He trained as a teacher and taught for many years in County Dublin.

John Masefield (1878–1967), poet, playwright and novelist, was born in Herefordshire. He joined the navy at fifteen, worked for some years in New York and spent the latter part of his life in England writing about the sea and the countryside. He was appointed Poet Laureate in 1930.

Thomas Moore (1779–1852) was born in Dublin. A musician and writer of patriotic and often nostalgic songs, he was very celebrated in his own day, in Dublin and in London. Among his more famous songs are 'The Last Rose of Summer' and 'The Minstrel Boy'.

Antaine Ó Reachtaire (1784–1835) is one of the most remarkable of Irish poets. Born near Kiltimagh in County Mayo, he was blinded by smallpox at the age of nine and had to spend most of his life as a beggar, playing the violin and composing poems on local people and events.

Seán Ó Ríordáin (1917–77) was born in Ballyvourney, County Cork, where he spent his youth. He lived most of his life in Cork city. His poetry is philosophical and spiritual by nature, and is characterised by a depth of thought and an intensity of feeling.

Padraic H. Pearse (1879–1916) was born in Dublin. He learned Irish in Rosmuc, Connemara, and wrote poems, stories and plays in both Irish and English. He founded St Enda's School in Rathfarnham and edited *An Claidheamh Soluis*, the weekly journal of the

Gaelic League. He played a prominent part in the formation of the Irish Volunteers and was executed for his part in the Easter Rising of 1916.

Joseph Mary Plunkett (1887–1916) was born in Dublin, the son of Count Plunkett. He learned Irish from his friend Thomas MacDonagh. As a member of the Irish Republican Brotherhood, he joined the Irish Volunteers, and was executed in Kilmainham Gaol for his part in the 1916 Rising. He married the artist Grace Gifford in jail the night before his execution.

Sir Walter Scott (1771–1832) was born in Edinburgh and studied law. It was the Border countryside in Scotland that provided the background for most of his writing. 'The Lay of the Last Minstrel' was his first major narrative poem and it proved to be hugely popular. In 1814 he published *Waverley,* the first of his historical novels, which was an immediate success.

Robert Louis Stevenson (1850–94) was born in Edinburgh. He battled against tuberculosis all his life and travelled in Europe and America in search of health. He died on the island of Samoa in the South Seas. He is most famous as the author of *Treasure Island, Kidnapped, Dr Jekyll and Mr Hyde* and the volume of poetry entitled *A Child's Garden of Verses.*

John Millington Synge (1871–1909) was born near Dublin and was of Anglo-Irish background. He was educated in Trinity College Dublin and spent some years in Paris, where he met W. B. Yeats. On Yeats's suggestion he spent much time in the Aran islands in order to write about Irish peasant life in Hiberno-English. Among his most famous plays are *Riders to the Sea* and *The Playboy of the Western World.*

Alfred Lord Tennyson (1809–92) was born in Lincolnshire, where his father was a rector. He studied at Cambridge. His first volume of poems included 'The Lady of Shalott' and 'The Lotos-Eaters'. His most famous work is 'In Memoriam', a series of elegies on the sudden death of his best friend, in which he grapples with the concept of immortality. He also wrote '*Morte d'Arthur*' and 'Ulysses'. Tennyson was made Poet Laureate in 1850.

Katharine Tynan (1861–1931) was born in Dublin. She loved reading and writing poetry, especially poems that were religious in theme, about the beauty of nature. She joined the Ladies' Land League and entertained such leading figures as Michael Davitt, John O'Leary and Douglas Hyde in her home. In 1893 she married Henry Albert Hinkson, a writer and classical scholar. She died in Wimbledon in 1931.

John Greenleaf Whittier (1807–92), a famous poet of the Americn Civil War, was born of Quaker parents in Massachusetts. He was an ardent abolitionist. A prolific and popular poet, he wrote many volumes of verse on political and rural themes.

Charles Wolfe (1791–1823) was born in County Kildare. He studied at Trinity College Dublin and became a clergyman of the Church of Ireland, taking up his first appointment in Donaghmore, County Tyrone. He is principally remembered as the author of the celebrated ode, 'The Burial of Sir John Moore', first published in the *Newry Telegraph*. He died of tuberculosis in Queenstown, County Cork.

William Wordsworth (1770–1850) was born in the Lake District of England and devoted his life to poetry. With Coleridge, he published the highly influential *Lyrical Ballads* in 1798. Wordsworth, one of the greatest of the Romantic poets, found much of the inspiration for his poetry in the wild countryside of his native Cumberland.

Index of Poets

Index of Titles

Index of First Lines